THE
HAPPY
HUMANIST

THE
HAPPY
HUMANIST

A LOOK AT THE MYSTERY OF THE SELF

GIL HOGG

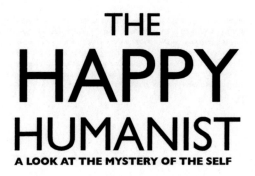

Matador
5 Weir Road
Kibworth Beauchamp
Leicester LE8 0LQ, UK
Tel: (+44) 116 279 2299
Fax: (+44) 116 279 2277
Email: books@troubador.co.uk
Web: www.troubador.co.uk/matador

ISBN 978 1848766 983

British Library Cataloguing in Publication Data.
A catalogue record for this book is available from the British Library.

Typeset in 12pt Bembo by Troubador Publishing Ltd, Leicester, UK

Matador is an imprint of Troubador Publishing Ltd

Printed in Great Britain by the MPG Books Group, Bodmin and King's Lynn

CONTENTS

INTRODUCTION

This is a simple book for ordinary people who wish to find greater enjoyment and peace in their lives.

I'm not referring to our lifetime goals and purposes; these will all be different. What I'm writing about is the happiness we have in our own small, personal world as we pursue our different goals. It's the comfort zone around us.

We all seek happiness, about which millions of words have been written. We know it's not easy to attain. We reach out, but we can't always quite grasp hold. Our enjoyment of life appears to be determined by our ability to manage a balance between what we want and what life is likely to send our way. If we get that balance right, life can be very enjoyable. If we get it wrong, it's miserable. This book is about that balance as an attitude.

Happiness is related to who we think we are. My thinking starts with our personal happiness because life only exists as far as it is consciously reflected in our mind. And each of us is unique; it's a marvellous thought about our potential. But working out who we think we are in a realistic way is a difficult task.

There is a vast chasm between our intellect and our capacity for self-judgment. We can split the atom, send a man to the moon and invent antibiotics, but we can't get on with Grandma. Our marriages often end in divorce, our partnerships in recriminations. We don't like our boss, and we still fight wars with other nations.

In our lives there is always a contrast between the fine things we can do with our reason and the uncertain, even chaotic (and sometimes wonderful) state of our human relationships. Understanding why human relationships are so often troubled, and the link with who we think we are, is a key to happiness.

Happiness implies genuine kindness, compassion and generosity toward others. The engine which drives us is our will to survive and prosper, but naked self-interest only brings anxiety and strife. It's ironic that the self-interest which can create our happiness needs to embrace kindness, compassion and generosity toward others.

Happiness is based on insight into the unpredictability of life. If we can understand and accept how unpredictability always affects the things we want, and what a force it is in our lives, we can develop the tolerance essential for a calm and enjoyable environment.

What do we mean by happiness? The humanist groups in a number of countries share a logo depicting 'the happy man', because they believe that happiness lies in the direction of freedom, reason, ethics and justice. Few people would quarrel with that. It is important that these concepts should be connected with happiness. A person who is oppressed cannot be happy.

We can have spa baths, massages, yoga classes, and take 'me-time'; they make us feel good – for a while. But happiness, as distinct from pleasure, is not a sensual thrill of the moment, it is a personal attitude.

Happiness is the personal attitude which seeks to create an environment of enjoyment and calm *in the mind*, as well as in our external life. We can be happy even though we are dealing with the conflicts in our life.

✸Chapter 1✸

CAN WE KNOW OURSELVES?

Our happiness is related to who we think we are, because everything we ask from life is dependent on who we think we are. If we get our self-image right, or nearly right, we'll be asking for things that life can deliver, and we won't be disappointed. If we can remain aware that we have no criteria for self-judgment, we can be cautious in forming our wants and expectations.

Who we think we are

$\mathcal{E}$verything about our peace and happiness seems to depend on *who* we think we are. We have a picture of ourselves, a self-image. It guides us towards what we think we're entitled to. The electrician's needs are going to be different from the banker's or the biochemist's. Actually, every single individual's needs are going to differ if only in detail. But within the comfort zone of each individual, it works out in the same way: 'I deserve this.' 'I'm entitled to that.' 'This is mine.' 'What I require is…' These 'wants' define us, and if they are achieved, we're pleased.

And of course, we don't often get exactly what we've been anxious about getting. We're disappointed. It's a double hit. Anxiety before, and disappointment afterwards.

Who we think we are, our self-image, may guide our wants, and make our disappointments sharper, but there is a remarkable problem with the concept of the self.

Philosophers have been trying for centuries to understand it! The psychologist CG Jung described the mystery of the human psyche as an insoluble puzzle and an incomprehensible wonder. It's incredible that we can send a rocket to the moon, but we're not very good at judging ourselves or other people. We can do amazing things with reason and logic, but our human relationships are unpredictable and often disastrous.

A starting point on the road to happiness is to understand why it is difficult to form an accurate self-image, and how the self-image works, or deceives us.

(1) Knowing ourselves and knowing other people

*If we are conscious of the difficulty of knowing ourselves accurately, we can be cautious about what we want from life. Happiness is asking for what we **can** have.*

The self as a certainty

At times, we're inclined to think of our self-image as a specific *thing*. We get a little weathered, but we go on from day to day, more or less the same. In a society which focuses so much on the personality of the individual, this idea of the self-image as a nugget of certainty is understandable. We have our individual name and address, our passport, our credit card, our bank account. We may even have an official title arising from our work, such as controller, manager or doctor. In this obvious factual respect, there is no doubt about our identity.

However, there is another aspect; 'us' in the wider

sense, as individuals interacting with others in all the manifold relationships we have with other people in our lives, from childhood to old age. This relates to our personality, what we are *like* as individuals.

The image we want to present

A person may present himself as ten different people in the course of a day, depending upon who he is meeting. If he visits a sick person in hospital he is kindly and sympathetic, but he isn't like that all the time. The image he shows to the man trying to sell him a new computer is different from the one he shows to his children. And the persona he reveals to a friend may yet be different again.

As people age and change with experience they have lots of reasons for wishing to present a different image of themselves to different people. They change these presentations from time to time to suit their own purposes. A politician may decide, for example, that when on television, he should appear quietly confident, rather than strident. A doctor may assume a 'beside manner.' A clerk may be particularly respectful in the presence of the managing director.

This may have been what CG Jung meant when he described the 'persona' we present to others as a kind of mask, designed to make a definite impression upon other people, and in effect attempting to conceal the nature of the individual.

What about what other people think of us?

When we think about it, we have to accept that everybody will see us differently, depending upon how well they know us, and where we stand in relation to them. To our young children we're a parent before anything else; to somebody else we may be an adviser, or a boss, and they see us primarily in that role. One acquaintance will find us kind and friendly, another may think we're abrupt or cold.

So many factors are changing here; the persona we present to others, the role in which we're seen and those who are judgmental over us.

Why not disregard other people's views?

Can we judge ourselves and disregard the confusing views of other people? One has to doubt whether this is possible if we want a reasonably accurate solution.

The picture of who we think we are, our self-image, is inextricably tied up with our perception of what other people think of us. Our self-image seems to be a judgment that we have made about *ourselves in relation to others*; a reflection or a measurement of us against them. Do we feel that we're viewed as competent in our job by those we're working with? How do friends see us as a husband or wife? Are we thought of as more influential than our peers or less so? Are we considered by those in our community to be more prosperous or less? Do we have a reputation for being smarter than others, or not so smart? Are we seen as fair-minded? Are we respected for our achievements? Are we regarded as a 'decent' person?

The puzzle of the self-image

All these very different points of view, of or from different people, as we assess them, become parts of the puzzle that is our own self-image.

This is where the problem is! We have to bear in mind that just as we present our different personas to others, so they present their different personas to us. In the hundred different ways that we may meet people, from cab-driver, to teacher, to business colleague, to lover, we reveal a different slant of ourselves, and so do those whom we meet. It's a confused basis on which to form a self-image, and very liable to be inaccurate. There are no reliable criteria here. There is no calculus or geometry which will give us an answer.

Our view of who we are, in the sense in which the phrase is used here, can only be based on impression, emotion and guesswork. It might be based on an opinion poll if a person happens to be a politician!

It seems to be a reasonable conclusion that we can't *really* know other people accurately enough to judge what they think of us. And the judgments we make about others are often made en masse. 'I think the people I work with regard me as rather skilful.' 'I'm sure I'm popular enough to be voted on to the committee at the golf club.' There will always be varied opinion within these groups, whom we judge as a whole. Our conclusion about our skills, popularity or reputation has no firm basis. We may or we may not make a reasonably accurate guess.

Surely we know the people close to us?

And this inability to know and understand must also apply to our closest friends and relations. We may feel we know our children or our parents, and in many ways we do, but we could only know them fully and completely if we were inside their mind.

There will always be hidden places we don't know about in people close to us. There will be reactions that are not fully communicated to us, or unexpected attitudes which we never knew about, and can't agree with, or accept as reasonable. Some parents, for example, will question the school subjects or career chosen by their child, and ultimately parent and child may have to view each other as 'on different wavelengths'. One family member cannot 'understand' how another could be so mean or extravagant about a wedding or a funeral. We have probably all heard somebody say, 'I never really knew my father' and yet the speaker may have spent his childhood and youth under the same roof. The essence of family disputes is often the unexpected attitude of a member. People, particularly family members, surprise us by revealing views of themselves which we didn't know existed.

We can observe that people, and groups of people, whether in families, jobs, clubs, churches or politics, are constantly moving through different phases of affection or disaffection for each other. The actions and attitudes which these fluctuating emotions project are a mire on which to try to build a self-image, but there is no other foundation.

In all our human relationships we struggle with the moving quicksand of emotion. The question always is, 'How am I regarded in this?' and it's a difficult question to answer with any precision.

The distorting window-glass of self-image
A person's self-image, who he thinks he is, constructed from an assessment of the people in his community in

relation to him, is made, as it were, through a window with distorting glass, and can never be particularly clear.

We have to accept – reluctantly – that we can misjudge how our skills are viewed, our reputation, our influence upon others, our importance in the community, our significance to our friends and our place in the affection of others, all as a result of the distorting glass – this inability to assess accurately the views and qualities of other people in relation to us.

We can often recognise a distorted self-image in others, but not so easily in ourselves. 'Who does he think he is?' we ask about somebody we find obnoxious. At the same time we might know, or at least suspect, that our own vision of ourselves might be flawed.

Are we really as good or bad as we think we are?

If a person tries to analyse his self-image as honestly as he can, he is likely to find that it is fraught with doubts. 'Am I *really* as capable as I think? So successful in my job? As well-liked as I think I am? Am I going to be supported if I stick my neck out here?' 'Is my reputation solid enough?' The answer often has to be that he isn't sure. And he ought to be equally doubtful when he's putting himself down. 'Am I such a loser?' The answer again has to be that he can't be sure.

Everything is uncertain about our self-image.

Could we give up trying to find ourselves?

The self-image is therefore a much more indistinct *thing* than we sometimes think. A person is a mix of different thoughts, emotions and actions from one day to another. When he says, as people sometimes do, 'I have to find myself,' or 'I need time to realise my true self,' it's fair to question whether there is anything tangible to find. Sure, he can acquire skills and perform tasks. Yes, he can be identified as a named individual, and no doubt he can be generally known and imprecisely tagged as good, nasty, ruthless, or clever, but he's behind a mask all the time, and he can have many masks. We are sometimes shocked by what we see as the inconsistencies in people we thought we knew.

Does it matter if our self-image is awry?

It's not so troubling that our self-image is likely to be awry if everybody else has the same problem. We can look with a certain scepticism at the over-large egos of the politicians and community leaders who are confidently telling us what to do, and the self-important people in every rank of society. And we can understand more readily how human relations can become confused and difficult, when people can't really know each other.

Are we entitled to what we're asking for?

Understanding that our self-image is not a solid object, but a foggy notion, merged in the confusion of both our own and other people's views of us, can make us less concerned about answering the unanswerable question: *'Who am I?'* It can also make us cautious in what we ask from life.

We ask things (or make demands) of our children, our wife or husband, our parents, our employees, our work-mates, our bosses, our friends; we ask people to vote for us if we're a politician. All these demands arise from who we think *we* are, and depend on what we think *we're entitled* to ask.

We have a problem. The problem is whether we're really entitled to what we're asking for; if we are, that's fine. If we're not, we'll face conflict and disappointment.

Weighing up relationships

Working out whether we are really entitled to something we want, often takes us into the sensitive territory of weighing up relationships. 'Should I expect my wife to accompany me on this journey?' 'Should I expect her to clean the house without assistance?' 'Should I insist that the children go to this school rather than that?' 'Am I justified in complaining about the new staff at the office?' 'Am I justified in expecting my friend to detour and give me lift in his car?' Such cases can cause unpleasant stresses and strains on us (and others) if we get them wrong. And we are making many more varied demands on others every week because we feel entitled so to do. It's desirable to keep in mind the fragility of relationships when we are pressing our perceived entitlements.

In the ordinary conflicts we face every day, such sensitivities may not apply, (say) an argument with a car dealer or a travel company where we believe they are resisting our rights. The question is how far, and just how hard we are going to push. There's a downside to this kind of situation too, in terms of stress, if we demand too much.

Conclusion

We cannot achieve happiness unless we bear in mind that we have difficulty judging ourselves accurately, and therefore question, and go on questioning as a habit, what we want from life and believe we're entitled to. Happiness is asking for what we expect and can reasonably have.

(2) The peculiarity of being conditioned

Conditioning tends to define 'our way' of doing things. Happiness depends upon understanding that 'our way' is one of a number of ways, not necessarily right, but merely different, and it depends on respecting those different ways.

Being conditioned means that we respond to situations by habit or training, rather than by working out a fresh response. The impact of conditioning upon our lives is profound; and it can make us into anything from angels to demons. Mostly, it just makes us different – our particular childhood like no other, our particular school, our particular language, the country where we were born.

Habit and training make life easier

Habit and training clearly make our lives easier, and account for many of the routines we follow every day in matters like diet, dress and manners; but above the very personal level of such routines, conditioning necessarily affects the formation of our thoughts.

Our conditioned thinking

We may seldom think of our race, religion, culture, nationality, class, political affiliations, school, university, employment, and family life in terms of the habits we develop, and the training we receive. But we can recognise that these are all formative experiences, which have imprinted themselves upon us, and conditioned us to some immeasurable extent in the way that we react. We may believe we're thinking in a free, unbiased way; but are we?

Conditioning and our self-image

It is difficult for us to get a clear view or understanding of our self-image, when we are conditioned by the peculiarities of our upbringing and environment, in ways which we would find hard to define accurately. We may be aware of some obvious aspects, like whether we are thinking as a Catholic, a Muslim, or an atheist, but there are a vast number of conditioning pressures, big and small, upon each one of us. We are therefore different from other people as a result of this conditioning, but just how different we can't be sure.

The conditioned background of a person can be very complicated, and the interaction between elements of it (say, for example) school, political affiliation, race, and religion, can be unclear.

Our various conditioned 'roles'

In trying to work out who we are, we may identify with some particular role which we have, often our job; army officer, nurse, business executive, schoolteacher. An army officer may look at a problem in a directive way as a disciplinarian; a nurse dealing with the same problem may be more concerned with human suffering. While our attitude will be influenced by conditioning in our role, we can, *if we are aware* and if we wish, move our thoughts beyond these conditioned positions. But we may well start in any situation, deeply influenced by our conditioned role.

Conditioning tends to define 'our way'

In an age of instant communication and mobility between communities, the deep cultural differences between groups of people seem more apparent to us; probably because differences of religious practice, language, diet, dress and other customs are no longer seen at a distance. These 'different' people are living in our street; and they have their own conditioned way of doing things. Our gut reaction to them may be uncomfortable. Consequently, the potential friction between our way of life and theirs is increased, and we have to work out ways to reduce it if we want to avoid that friction and live in harmony.

If we are aware of our susceptibility to conditioning – although it's unavoidable in some form – we can see that 'our' way is one of a number of ways, not necessarily right, but merely different. It follows that if we want to maintain peaceful intercourse, we have to make space for other 'ways' apart from ours.

The unthinking effects of conditioning

At different times, whole nations can become subservient to ideas, political beliefs and institutions because of the propensity of people to be conditioned. We saw this in World War II. People may serve 'the party,' 'the company,' 'the regiment,' 'the family,' even 'the club,' and these dedications are not necessarily wrong; but it is an advantage to have the insight that we can be *trained* to take a certain view, support a position, or perform a task, without actually questioning whether it's right.

The insight that we may be responding to a situation as a result of habit and training can motivate us to rethink our position and try to make a fresh response.

The conditioning effect of the market place

We must also be conditioned by our experience every day. We evolve individually as we are influenced. We are conditioned for example, to accept that certain possessions will distinguish us from other people; they suggest, if we own them, that we have money and taste and style; they tend to give us a superior self-image.

The crude idea that we are superior to somebody else because we drive an expensive car is easy to reject, but the fact is that a self-image can be built up by a multiplicity of such crudities. If we owned expensive cars, jewellery, and houses, we'd surely get a buzz out of it; that feeling of distinguishing ourselves from other people in a pleasant way. We may think we're better than others in the sense of being more capable or successful, even while our more thoughtful side is saying, 'You're being a fool. This reasoning is false.'

Who we think we are seems to owe much to emotion, and very little to rationality.

The bias of habit and training

The effect of our conditioning then is that we each have this very particular peculiarity, which in lots of conscious and unconscious ways affects our judgment of others and therefore of ourselves.

There's little doubt that our conditioning can work

unconsciously on our responses. The experiences that we have lived through produce attitudes in us in ways that we may hardly notice. We don't ask to be trained and moulded by life. It happens. We may have endured hell as a soldier, poverty as a child, or suffered serious and permanent injury in a car accident. These experiences, and many which are less harrowing, will mark our decision-making in ways that are indefinable unless we think very carefully.

When a person has to make a decision, he probably doesn't often reflect, 'I'm thinking along these lines because I'm trained as an engineer,' or 'because I was brought up in a rural society' or 'because of my race,' and then question whether that is the right approach. It's also too complicated at the moment of decision to tease out all the *other* conditioning factors which are operating at the same time, such as (say) schooling and parenting. Nor does he necessarily have time in a busy life. He simply reacts.

On the occasions when we do analyse our self-image at the moment of decision, we can sometimes see the bias of our habit and training.

While it is also true that conditioning by institutions like churches or learned professions will place people in groups who are likely to think along similar lines, everybody's conditioning must vary to a greater or lesser degree. We all absorb our different experiences in our own unique way. We get a sense of the astonishing diversity of people.

Conclusion
Conditioning is an aspect of our uniqueness as individuals.

We can bear in mind that it can make us press perhaps unreasonably or unconsciously for 'our way'. To have an environment of calm in which we can enjoy life, it follows that we have to respect other ways of doing things.

(3) Being Unique

Our uniqueness is our most wonderful and fruitful characteristic as a species. With the solitariness of being unique comes our fundamental responsibility for our own life, and the implicit need to recognise the individuality of others.

Locked in our cell of experience

Sometimes there are as many views about an issue as there are people to express them, and this is a reminder of our uniqueness and of the difficulty in human relations. Nobody else can be inside our skin, fully sharing our reaction to events, however close to us they may be. We are locked in our own cell of experience.

The difficulty with words and actions

We know, and can sometimes feel, our words and actions are imprecise and indistinct. We could probably write a treatise on our thoughts and feelings about our relationship with a person we love, and still fall short of fully expressing ourselves. We can also perform all sorts of acts to show kindness and loyalty, and again *feel* that they are limited in conveying exactly what we mean.

The problem of communicating completely

It follows that however close we are to a parent, a child or a friend, we can never communicate fully and precisely our own unique view of life. We can talk, we can write books, we can perform acts which demonstrate our feelings; but we can never precisely pass on the myriad of thoughts and feelings which come to us in each moment of our experience. In our ability to communicate precisely and completely, there always seems to be some residue, unspoken, unwritten, unexpressed, incommunicable.

Poets, novelists, artists, playwrights, musicians and film-makers will take the communication of human experience and sensibility as far as words, pictures and music can go; but it seems to fall short of communicating the *whole* complexity of a person's intimate personal experience. James Joyce made a heroic attempt to communicate that complexity in Ulysses, but the limitations of the written word are obvious.

We can regard this, not as a problem, but as part of the beauty and wonder of our lives, because it leaves open the possibility that new and valuable insights about ourselves and other people are always there to be revealed.

The solitariness of being unique

We shouldn't be downhearted about being alone inside our mind. We can celebrate our uniqueness; it's a glorious fact of life. We're different from everybody else! Everybody! Neither better or worse, but different. This knowledge can give us a feeling of calm confidence.

Being alone inside our mind is also a reminder that we alone have to deal with the worries which affect us. We have to make our way in life as a result of experience gathered through our senses. Whether we decide to be a gardener, a surgeon or a beachcomber is our decision. It doesn't matter if we are talked into it. It doesn't matter whether we are so conditioned in our upbringing that our following hardly seems like a decision at all, just a natural happening. The result is the same. We have decided or accepted or acquiesced in a way to take our life forward. We must be responsible (in the sense of being answerable) for that action. We have to take the blame or the glory for what happens to us.

In the same way, we are responsible for the myriad of decisions we make every day as we go about our affairs, important or trivial – how we speak to people, how we deal with them, how we conduct ourselves. The majority of people understand this everyday responsibility very well, but it is perhaps not so easy to see our fundamental and overall responsibility for the shape of our own life.

We can certainly blame other people for pressing us to take one route rather than another. Most of us come under pressure from family, friends, our culture, our race or religion, and this pressure can determine the course of our life. But in the end we have to accept responsibility for that course. We have followed it or submitted to it. It's ours, even if we believe there is a source of strength outside us, God, man or a guiding star.

Can we accept responsibility for ourselves?

When help, or pressure, comes to us from outside, from friends, family, and institutions within our community, we have to deal with that help, we have to assess it, try to understand it, and react to it, and how we do so is up to us. If a person has religious faith, he has *decided or accepted*

17

that he has faith, even if he acquired faith initially as a result of conditioning.

So with our remarkable uniqueness, comes not only the solitariness of being unique, but for all of us, the responsibility for dealing with our whole lives. It is going to include situations which nobody else upon the planet can ever share *fully* or understand in the way we do.

Uniqueness and who we think we are

How does our uniqueness affect our self-image? Unfortunately, by confliction. It was suggested in the first section that we can't see each other clearly. The second described our conditioned viewpoint. Our uniqueness adds the additional difficulty that people can't communicate fully and completely.

Our mutual understanding is easily blurred, but more than that, this is a recipe for the friction and strife in human relations which is all too evident. It suggests we should be as non-judgmental as we can about other people, and try to see their viewpoint. This thought, in action, tends to lead us away from conflict and encourages a peaceful environment.

It is also clear that since human relations are so imprecise, we cannot find any criteria either for self-judgment, or the judgment of other people. There is nothing in our individual human relationships and connections which makes them measurable. A parent can't examine his or her relationship with a son with arithmetical precision. There is no formula which can be applied to measure one's standing with the supervisor at the office. There is no equation which will work out the quality of our love for another person. It's all impression and guesswork, fraught with the likelihood of error.

We can certainly claim, 'This is me.' But what are we talking about? Not merely our physical body, or our literal identity. We have to include our mind. What is 'me-like' about one's mind? Nothing precise. We could list ten qualities we think we have. Alternatively, we might list twenty or a hundred and twenty! But 'me' isn't simply a list of qualities. 'Me' is a persona which manifests itself in action in ways which can be difficult to guess or anticipate.

Is our self-image guess-work?

Of course in practice we *do* have a view of ourselves. We form a self-image by ignoring the difficulties, and assuming that our judgment of ourselves in relation to others is more or less right, but that unfortunately doesn't make it right. We are peering through that distorting window glass.

Not for a moment can one suggest that we shouldn't indulge in this guess-work. It's natural to do so. But it seems a good idea, at the same time, for us to question who we think we are, and to do so frequently, if only to dislodge ideas which look like hardening into certainties.

Ideally the time to ask the questions, *Who do I think I am?* And *Have I got it right*? is before we start wanting something, and at least at a moment when our expectations are defeated. That could be a number of times in the average day!

Conclusion

Being unique and responsible for ourselves is both a

cause for personal celebration and implicitly requires us to recognise the individuality of other people, because they too have the same qualities.

(4) Virtual reality and the psychonet

Our mind and senses don't give us an absolutely accurate view of what is happening outside us. This is another reason to be cautious about misunderstanding others.

The limitations on our ability to understand what's 'out there'

It's plain that we can only know what our own unique senses tell us. What's happening outside our skin, is what we *think* is happening. This is not solipsism (the belief that the self is the only knowable thing); it is simply a practical observation about the limitation on our ability to receive and understand information from outside sources. There is evidence of autonomous external causes 'out there' beyond us and hence there appears to be a reality beyond our mind; but it remains true that we can only receive the version of it which our mind and senses allow.

It follows too, that because other people have their view of what is outside them, ours may not necessarily be correct – only different.

What we can perceive is dependent on the quality of our particular mind and senses. Two people climb Mt Fuji together, and each has a different experience. Two people go to watch Hamlet at the same theatre, and each will come away with different impressions. Their individual perceptions will obviously be affected by education, past experience, and the strength and health of the mind and senses. But the net result will be two different views. There might be many similarities, but there are likely to be many differences. The scene is set, even with the best intentions, for confusion, misunderstanding and even argument. We misunderstand what other people are doing and saying in relation to a particular external issue all the time.

Virtual reality

What we perceive with our mind and senses can be likened to the virtual reality created by a computer. Imagine a person sitting in a room browsing the internet on a screen. He sees the world via this screen, and learns as a result. He interacts with others, as we do on the web, via this screen; it is how he – and we – are in touch with others. The analogy is used because it puts the imperfections of the screen, and ourselves as operators, *between* us and what we think of as objective reality.

It's worth thinking about the screen between ourselves and what's going on 'out there.' It raises the question in many cases whether we really do understand what is happening with sufficient clarity, and argues against snap judgments and fixed positions.

The connection between human minds and knowledge

The psychonet, a suggested name for the connection between human minds and knowledge, emphasises the potentiality of human minds to be connected, as if we are all connected through an internet. And the connection between people (and between people on the internet) is not limited to trivial communication, but embraces the exchanging, recording and refining of information, the accumulation of knowledge, and a powerful influence upon opinion, which leads, in turn, to changes in our way of life.

It's almost impossible to continue thinking about the psychonet without considering its effect in terms of social development, and looking at human beings *and* their collective knowledge as one whole exponentially developing process.

Vast technical and scientific progress has been made in the last hundred years, and the pace of change seems to increase year by year. Changes in medicine and gadgetry don't, in themselves, lead to improvements in human relations, but there is an aspect of this advance which does: closer communication and involvement between people globally, and the exchange of information, must take us closer to understanding each other.

This process is dealt with in a little more detail in Chapter 5. It is one that is arguably heading in the right direction for us as peace, justice and freedom point the rational way toward an environment where it is possible to enjoy our shared life.

Conclusion

The previous four somewhat overlapping sections have considered the mystery of the 'self'. In summary:

1. Our self-image depends on what we think other people think of us, but we can't assess them accurately, and similarly they can't assess us because we present different and changing personas to each other.

2. We are conditioned by our own peculiar personal experience of life which slants our thought toward 'our way'.

3. We are each unique and alone inside our head and can't communicate fully and completely with anybody, or they with us.

4. And we have access only to a possibly flawed virtual reality through our senses.

Viewing conflicting human relationships in a different way

If we can be aware of our lack of capacity for accurate self-judgment, and aware of the mystery of the self, we are on the threshold of viewing the turmoil and the confusion of human relationships in a different way.

First, we can understand that the very nature of the self makes for misunderstanding, and hence conflict in human relations becomes a very natural and likely event.

Second, we can approach these conflicts in a more objective and detached way, and without feeling that we are victims of somebody else's unreasonableness.

Third, we can see that this insight is likely to enable us to resolve conflict more effectively.

The deleterious effect of the distorted self-image

A person with a distorted self-image can touch our life in deleterious ways; we think about national dictators, business moguls, politicians, bureaucrats, the boss at the office, the chairman of the club, a controlling parent. We have all at some time felt the ill effects of somebody else's maladjusted self-image. When the distortion becomes extreme we can recognise it, and ponder why what is obvious to us is apparently unseen by the person concerned. Of course at the same time, in some more modest way we could be making the life of somebody close to us, oppressive.

Our urge for a self-image

One of the curious contradictions here is that despite all the problems we may have with forming an accurate view of ourselves, we're nevertheless trying to do so all the time. We yearn to distinguish ourselves from our fellows. If a person *believes* he is smarter, richer, or more powerful than others, he feels superior and secure. It is important to all of us, for our wellbeing, that we think we're surviving quite successfully, and that we are well thought of by our peers. This urge to distinguish ourselves is a reflection of our *wanting,* our will to survive and prosper.

Are we actually more real than anybody else?

The natural trend of our thoughts sometimes is to believe that we are the centre of being, more real than anybody or anything else; this is normal self-centredness. Young children show this quality. With experience of the world comes a greater perspective on this childishness – the need to accommodate other people.

The incessant construction of the self-image

We can see that we are tirelessly constructing an image of who we are, and at the same time, partially blind in the material we use (because of this difficulty of judging ourselves or others accurately). The irony of the human personality is this incessant attempt to construct a self-image which is inherently and necessarily flawed.

And there is little satisfaction in this incessant attempt. We are a prey to anxieties. If a man has money, he feels good but wants more, or has anxiety about securing what he has. If he has power and influence, he's concerned that he might be weakened and must strengthen his position. If he thinks himself clever, he wonders whether he may be exposed in some way as mistaken, even slightly stupid. If he is pleased with his appearance, he seeks flattery to prove it, and wants to believe what he hears.

The self-image, the 'I am', is constructed on this quagmire of wanting more of something than we already have, or seeking constant reassurance that our position is not being undermined.

The difference with self-confidence

It isn't suggested that anybody should abandon self-confidence. On the contrary, we need it; well-founded self-confidence seems to be a virtue, and we all hope to have sufficient at the right time. Real self-confidence is usually about finite tasks and events around us. 'I'm confident I can manage this team,' 'I have trained to win this race,' 'I'm sure I'll pass this exam,' 'I can handle these difficult cases'. A person who is simply self-confident about everything as a kind of attitude to life, may be foolish.

Where is the ordinary person, then?

The unknowns and uncertainties of the self show us that we are trying to survive in what is likely to be a confusion of human relationships. This likelihood of confusion is something we have to be aware of in all our dealings with others, whether close family or distant politicians. We can see the problems of those who become preoccupied with their self-image, and deluded by what they see. We may hopefully reach the conclusion that since we can never assess who we are accurately, we are going to be cautious about asserting what we think we're entitled to.

The half-blind leading the half-blind

We have the difficulty of self-judgment, but there is also the difficulty of judging other people in our many dealings with them. Politicians provide an extreme example of the problem. We have to elect politicians to govern us without knowing them, although we believe we know them sufficiently, and most of us would say we trust the person we vote for. They present their credentials publicly; they look and sound acceptable, and we agree with what we understand to be some of their views. But that's all. We don't and can't know them. We delegate to them the task of shaping our lives. Later we may find some of them cheating on their taxes, or acting in conflict of interest, or simply not doing what they pledged to do. They are just ordinary human beings with all the ordinary frailties. Can we trust them to act with integrity when they tell us that they will introduce a new law for our benefit?

It's an electorate of people with limited vision, us, electing people who have equally limited vision, and then being led by them. At work, it's the same. We don't know our bosses, and they don't know us. And these same confusions arise within the family and between friends.

The inability to know other people

Certainly, there are degrees of knowing other people, depending upon the closeness of relationships; but the area of the unknown and unknowable in each human being can be vast, whether family or friend. Thus, in dealings between human beings there are inevitably mistakes, misconceptions, wrong turns, u-turns, much absurdity and unfortunately, physical conflicts; perhaps on the worst view, a morass of myopic people pushing each other this way and that. Human relationships are an amazing contrast to the clarity of human mathematics.

This book is intended to be a realistic look at human psychology in action, not a pessimistic condemnation of human efforts. Balzac wrote a series of novels which he called 'The Human Comedy', depicting French society. We could equally describe human society as a tragedy or a farce. Certainly, there is much that we might want to disown, but if we look at the human struggle in its totality, if we look at the brilliant originality of it (the progress to where human-kind is today), if we look at the never-ending search for freedom and justice, we find a nobility which surpasses all the turmoil, confusion and human dishonesty.

The fact that we are each alone and responsible for ourselves, and do not, and cannot know other people fully, is a salutary reminder of our social limitations. It suggests the value of care, restraint, understanding and tolerance in our relationships, not for any moral or ethical reason, but very practically, to avoid mistakes and misunderstandings, to enable each of us to live in a more effective and harmonious way – and create the conditions for happiness.

The advantage of not being 'me'

We all have the same characteristic of tending to be self-centred, and it's a whole lot easier to liberate ourselves from the pressure of self-centredness when we understand how prone to error it is. The world from the standpoint of 'me' is a very tense and stressful one. Are we getting what we're entitled to? And what if we're not?

As soon as we understand that our wanting and our sense of entitlement can be a source of anxiety and unhappiness, we can choose to adjust our wants, and then relax and enjoy life more fully. We can actually survive more successfully in this way than by clinging to our unjustified wants.

If we were to feel regret and depression at our conclusions about the 'non-self' because *nobody really knows me'*, or *'nobody can understand me'*, or *'I'm all alone and isolated'* we would be sliding into that swamp of misconception where the self-image lurks. Everything to do with 'I', 'me', 'what I want', or 'what I'm entitled to,' leads back to who we think we are, and the illusion of our self-image. It needs to be constantly questioned.

The happiness of being unknowable

It is the very fact that we are unknown and unknowable to ourselves and those connected with us, that can make our human relationships so fascinating and fruitful. We can always find new aspects of ourselves, and new aspects of our friends. It is the unknown depths of people which are so interesting, surprising and often creative, and which renew, and go on renewing relationships as we grow with experience and change.

Human beings are not characterized by the regular, by a conceptual average, by classified similarities, or by dimensions. Our most outstanding and wonderful quality is our uniqueness. It's a cause for joy and celebration!

✾ Chapter 2 ✾

'I WANT!'

In seeking happiness, an environment where we can experience peace and enjoyment, we are pursuing a selfish quest, but ironically one that necessarily implies genuine kindness, compassion and generosity toward others. Naked self-interest only brings us worry and strife.

Selfish?

A baby wants from the cradle. In every waking moment we have 'wants'. Wanting is as natural to us as breathing. We want a shower, a clean shirt, breakfast. We want love and affection. We want somebody, including the dog, to think we're pretty special. We have hundreds, thousands of little wants every day. We would probably agree that our big wants are likely to be good health, a happy family, a worthwhile job, and warm friends – a possible, but by no means the only framework for happiness.

The engine of our lives

The 'I want' feeling appears to be the engine of our lives. We strive to satisfy our wants, and to some extent at least, we succeed. It's the fact that we only succeed *to some extent* in getting what we want that seems to be the cause of unhappiness.

Our wants can be separated into categories which although rather inexact, may help us to see their significance more readily. We have above all the urge to *survive*. We need *security*. We pursue *pleasure* and *sexual expression*. We're attracted to *power* and control over others. And we search for *meaning*. These are discussed briefly to show a picture of what we're like as individuals.

As every person is unique, there will be a myriad of personal variations within the generality of these conclusions, *and* there will be some (very few) extraordinary people, saints or monsters who seem to be wired up in a different way to most of us, and don't conform to the sketched picture.

We want to live

We strive first to stay alive. We have survived disease, war and famine successfully as a species through the ages. If we are caught in rough seas we don't just give up and sink. We battle against snowstorms and hurricanes. We suffer starvation and torture. Those who have a mortal illness often extract every ounce of life left in their bodies before they surrender.

Our survival instinct, in its most elemental form, is expressed in this will to live even in the toughest circumstances.

But staying alive isn't enough

We don't want to merely stay alive; we want security. Without it we have no basis to find prosperity; and without security we are unlikely to find happiness, this environment of peace where we can enjoy our lives. Security is important to us at every level – the security of our personal relationships, security of our job, security from crime and disease, and the security of our country.

As community creatures, we satisfy so many of our security wants through the communities in which we live. We contribute to health services, street maintenance, rubbish removal, energy companies, the judiciary, the police and the army. These and many other community benefits like them are fulfilling our wants, maintaining our security, and promoting our better survival.

Our desire for pleasure

Pleasure is not only one of our important wants, it is an essential element of happiness – but only an element. If we could not move toward pleasure and away from pain, we would have a miserable, a scarcely endurable life. However, we have learned by hard experience that the desire for pleasure can conflict with our need to survive. Too much of certain kinds of pleasure can harm or even kill us. A surfeit of the pleasures induced by food, alcohol or drugs reduces us to ineffectiveness and pushes up the medical bills we have to pay. And so we have developed all sorts of ways of taking our pleasures without excess.

At the same time, there are so many sources of pleasure in music, art, literature, sport and friendship which are harmless and enhance our lives. We can enjoy a good conversation, or taking a walk in the country.

The pleasures of celebrity

People like and seek celebrity status. If a person can build up a self-image by being known to others for some achievement, he feels enlarged, important. We live in an age where television screens and the internet can offer a kind of celebrity very cheaply; people become well-known by being in front of the camera, their underlying 'achievement' if there was one, unknown or forgotten.

Being a celebrity may seem admirable, but the celebrity can't have any clearer vision of himself than we have of ourselves; it's treacherous ground. Celebrities may well feel more anxiety about their image than we do, because that is what they trade on; it's always a nagging case of 'what will people think?'

The question of who a celebrity thinks he is, is corrosive, not only because of personal anxiety about whether he's got it right, but also whether it has been or is being undermined by change – as it must be ultimately. It's sometimes embarrassing for us to watch the legion of fading actors, singers, and television personalities, often painfully trying to maintain or recreate an image which they think they might have had in the past.

The pleasures of celebrity are laced with pain. It would probably be fair to recognise that in some, probably very minor way, we could equally be the victim of such a position.

The pleasures of money

Money is a big want. A lot of people think money is the key to happiness; it certainly means a high degree of security from the world's ills. Obviously, unless we can afford food, clothing, shelter and health-care, it's difficult for us to have the relative ease which is an important basis for the enjoyment of life (but happiness is an *attitude* which is not necessarily dependent upon material ease).

Money also affects our self-image. If a person has more

money relative to others, his expectations are greater. A man with ten million pounds in the bank probably won't want to sit and wait his turn in the hairdressing salon, or drive a small Ford; and the wife of the owner of the local plastics factory may expect the best seat in the theatre. These people have the money, and their self-images tell them that they are 'entitled' to the advantages that they buy.

Is happiness about things or relationships?

At the same time, looking at the effect of money from a modest level of prosperity, it's clear that being relatively rich can't enable a person to avoid the pain and strain of ordinary life. Travelling first class, dining at exclusive restaurants, staying at luxury hotels, and unburdening a lot of the fiddling tasks of living on to servants may be pleasurable, but it can't absolve a person from the complexity of human relationships, for that is where the strain of our life lies. The worries we suffer every day arise less from *things,* from bricks, masonry, furniture and machines, than from our obligations to people, and from our relationships with family, friends, and colleagues.

In the 2008 world banking crisis, a few rich people who suffered huge losses committed suicide. It seems rather absurd, as well as sad, for a healthy and intelligent person to do this, but it's a case of not being able to face the perceived personal shame, the diminution of the self-image, which arises from having less money.

We can conclude that money may give us more choices, and we can buy a lot of exclusivity, material comfort and security with it, but beyond a *certain level* it isn't a key to the environment of peace that we seek; it can't greatly lessen our worries; it may just give us a slightly different set of worries.

The 'certain level' is something we can only set ourselves, keeping in mind this problem about who we think we are. We can be fooled into thinking that we *need* a lot of money to underline our importance and superiority. Actually, most of us can get along very well without wardrobes stuffed with clothes, and houses packed with the latest, soon to be redundant, consumer gadgets. A house in the Caribbean, a gold Rolex, or a Ferrari would be nice, but we're not going to suffer without them.

However, it remains true that we are conditioned to strive to achieve higher status and more money. The striving and struggling around money is understandable and to be expected.

We can make a distinction between the pleasures that money can give, and the worries that can't be bought off.

Our sexual expression and survival

We're often talking or reading about sexual practices, sexual habits, sexual scandals and diseases; it is a constant subject of interest for discussion. Sexual expression is something we want, and it can play an important part in our happiness. We see sexual connotations used to sell products like cars and clothes which superficially have nothing to do with sex. We can find elements of sexuality threaded through most of the plays, films and literature we have seen and read throughout our lives. More obviously, sexuality is reflected in customs, in laws, and in moral standards. Sex in its many aspects is therefore both overtly and covertly, present in our lives.

The sexual atmosphere in which we live, ultimately encourages pleasure as distinct from happiness; it also encourages procreation – an absolutely basic need for the survival of the species.

Why should we want to have power, control or influence over others?

Most of us would deny that we have an overt desire to exercise power over others; but if power, control and influence mean not only social and political power in the community, but also our power, control or influence over our family, those with whom we work, and our friends and acquaintances, then a different picture emerges.

Parents use their authority as such all the time; some never stop trying to use it. At work, seniority over colleagues brings advantages as well as satisfaction. We often learn how to persuade and influence our friends to our benefit. If we have a measure of power, control or influence over others, we can feel secure in many situations in our daily lives. And if our happiness is to be found in an environment of peace that we are free to enjoy, we will want a certain amount of control to sustain that environment.

Why does power corrupt?

That power does corrupt has never been seriously contested since Lord Acton is reported to have said so in 1887.

A person who has a measure of power is likely to feel entitled to the advantages it brings. The manager will have a bigger expense account than those who work for him, and he will be, to some extent, in charge of making the rules. He won't be as accountable and answerable as a person on the shop floor. He can 'get away' with things. He will argue that he isn't being dishonest like a thief, but merely doing what he is *entitled* to do. The sense of entitlement, justified by his consciousness of his own superior position, his self image, arises as a key element.

Bosses in big business have no doubt that they are entitled to their multi-million pound salaries although the salaries are completely disproportionate to the money they pay their employees. The question of a balance between what is paid to a boss and a worker rarely arises. The exploitation of the 'system' by those in power is simply what people in power do – whatever system we happen to be considering in business or politics and wherever in the world.

It may be that we are all inclined to have a sense of entitlement, as a result of our power, which is on the over-large side. The element of corruption creeps in because of the erroneous judgement about *what we* are entitled to. We can get this wrong very easily.

Loss of vision by those in power

The holding of power is frequently characterized by a loss of vision. In 2009, there was a public scandal about the personal expenses charged to the taxpayer by members of the British parliament, and their unfailing answer, having tried to keep the facts secret, was: 'We're entitled to make these charges.'

Although there was a rule book, rather dubiously

followed, there was actually a vast disparity between what members of parliament interpreted as their entitlement, and the public perception of what was fair. And yet the people claiming this entitlement were the law-makers, the custodians of the public conscience. For a long time they could not see why the public was so angry.

Perhaps the other aspect of the parliamentary scandal worth noting is that the objectionable behaviour was spread across members of parliament in all political parties. In other words, corruption is an infection which knows no ideology.

The germ of corruption seems to be implicit where people in power lose their vision, that is to say, have a deluded self-image. We have to admit that corruption is as alive and well in the developed west as it is in other places, but hopefully in a less flagrant fashion. Our vision of what we are entitled to justifies itself, wanting more benefits, often misjudging the propriety of the action, or miscalculating that the risk of securing a benefit is worth the reward.

It would be wrong to conclude that people are inherently corrupt; but our wants can produce a self-image which may make us undiscriminating and greedy. We can certainly misjudge what we are 'entitled' to.

We don't like giving up power

Another important aspect of power is that people don't like giving it up. People often cling to power when a rational assessment suggests that they should relinquish it. Parents are sometimes reluctant to give up power over their children, and they justify this with arguments about protecting the children and doing their duty as a parent.

The terrible effect that clinging to power can have at nation state level is well-known, but we have all probably felt its unhelpful and hurtful effects in the work-place, the social club and the family. Why?

Just as a person can feel diminished by being declared redundant at his work, so the people in our community who hold power feel insecure and diminished when faced with its possible surrender. They often react by holding on to their position for as long as possible. The chairman of the parish beautification society may be set to go on for another decade! As the adage has it, power resists divestment.

Being diminished by loss of power

The believed loss of status of, say, the man who retires from a corporate job where he is responsible for many people can be confusing and painful. He's not as important, useful or sought-after as he was. But this same diminution appears to apply as much to the ageing dictator as to the long serving secretary of the bowls club. They cannot see that in the eyes of others, they are past their best value; they cannot accept the idea that they ought to make room for somebody else with fresh ideas. Only their own ideas seem to be important. What is apparent to us all is that such people have 'lost sight' of themselves. Their self-image is skewed. 'Who do they think they are?' we ask.

Our search for meaning

The search for meaning at a variety of levels seems to be an unquenchable drive we all share, because knowing the answers can – we hope – ensure survival and security. Having a sense of meaning in our personal life is essential to happiness.

The need to understand a situation, and find a meaningful explanation whether at a personal, community, international or cosmic level is something we all share, but we obviously don't and couldn't delve into all these aspects of meaning ourselves. The meaning of the universe is in the hands of scientists and preachers; our culture rests with seats of learning. But if a person has a pain in the chest, he wants to know why. If the local council is proposing to take away half of his garden, he wants to know how they can do this lawfully. At a personal level, understanding the meaning of all the changes occurring around us is vital to our improved survival.

The search for meaning seems to be a very important aspect of our wants, and our happiness. Meaning and meaninglessness are discussed in more detail in Chapter 5.

It's difficult to admit that our wants are insatiable

What conclusions can we draw from these many wants of ours? There are many pleasures in life which we enjoy, but it is evident that our wants and expectations are seldom met precisely, or if they are, after a short time we usually want more, or something different. If we were *completely* satisfied all the time, we would be stupefied, we would lapse into torpor like a heroin addict or a drunk.

Our sensual satisfactions tend to be very short in relation to the hours in a day – a meal, listening to music, a drink, sexual intercourse. Other pleasures, too, tend to be short lived – reading a book, viewing a garden, going to a film. These activities are soon over, and afterwards, we want more, or we want to do something different.

There are times when we can become absorbed in a task for quite a long time, our work perhaps, painting a picture or writing a letter; this absorption, like meditation, is a desirable state. When it ceases we might have pleasant afterthoughts, but it's not long before our wants and expectations emerge as insatiably as ever.

'Things' don't seem to satisfy for long

If we consider the acquisition of 'things' like cars, houses, furniture and gadgets as a means of satisfaction, we have to admit that they give pleasure for a while, but it is not very long before the warm enthusiasm accompanying a new acquisition has faded, and we want these things slightly, or perhaps greatly different than they are. We wish we'd bought a car of a different colour, or with more power. We find our new house has disadvantages; the heating system is unreliable, the road outside is more noisy than we thought. Our new computer seems to have a mind of its own. And so it goes with everything we have. Wanting, and wanting something different or 'better.'

Is it dog-eat-dog?

If we have insatiable wants, is it a cruel dog–eat–dog world? We can see that nature is cruel, and we know about predatory behaviour in the animal world. At the same time, in the human world, millions of people are suffering the effects of war, famine and disease. We are aware that millions of children are born only to die when there are the means to save at least some of them. Cruelty to men, women and children is widespread in many political regimes. And then there is the cruelty of poverty.

We may be horrified when we see on the TV screen (viewed in our safe and secure home), the fate of the victims of civil war, tsunamis and earthquakes. There's an appeal for funds. We might give something; we want to think all those tortured people are getting *some* help. Then they can fade from our consciousness, as though they were no more real than the images on the TV screen which we found so disturbing.

It's not fair to say we avert our eyes from a great deal of that suffering, because so much of it is thrust upon us through the television screen, the internet and newspapers, that we couldn't tackle it personally, even if we wanted to. It's probable that even if we all devoted much of our personal resources to the less fortunate, we could never eliminate large-scale suffering; that would take an international consensus of unimaginably utopian proportions.

Instead we give to charities, and work for charities; we ask our politicians to end conflict, but to all this there is an unspoken proviso: whatever is done mustn't cost us too much. We need a certain amount of money to maintain our lifestyle, and we're very touchy about our taxes going up. We've probably worked hard, and we don't want what we believe to be our share of the good life to be diminished.

So life isn't quite dog-eat-dog, but it can be cruel and it's always unpredictable.

We would be fooling ourselves if we didn't admit that as individuals we're selfish. The community in which we live, people not too different from us, may well be selfish too in what it's prepared to vote for. It was President Clinton who, when asked what the issue in an election was, said, 'It's the economy, stupid!' In other words, 'How's the dollar in *my* pocket getting on?'

Can making a space for others facilitate our survival?

Today, the struggle for survival between individuals and between communities, which is still very crude in some parts of the world, has become a refined process in others. It doesn't mean kill and plunder for us; if it did, our survival would not be assured; we would live in violence. What seems to have been learned over the centuries in the west is that survival is better ensured by accommodating others, making space for them.

The different peoples of the human race have chosen to mix themselves up, rather than segregate themselves on islands or continents or behind walls; they intermarry and trade and form alliances between communities and nations. The result is that we have had to share the services of *our* community with people of other races, religions and nationalities.

The sharing of goods (to some extent) is not a soft option for us, or an act of generosity; it is the price of peace; it is necessary for our survival, and necessary ultimately to create the conditions for our happiness.

We know as a simple fact that a person whom we might regard as a 'foreigner' or an alien is nevertheless a unique individual. We have to treat him or her as an individual, or beggar our own intelligence by denying what *we* are. We are compelled to look at the rights we accord ourselves, and then deal with the question of what rights we should give the 'foreigner' or alien. We have learned too from our historical experience that with slavery and oppression comes its inseparable shadow, rebellion and violence. The pathway to peace, and the implication of sharing become obvious – although we sometimes advance on the path somewhat reluctantly.

Man in a state of nature

The philosopher Thomas Hobbes said that man lives in a state of nature, a war of all against all, and in an abstract but nevertheless very real sense, this appears to be true today. However, in the society in which we live, the 'war' works through many refinements. At international level, a network of treaties protect our country's territorial interests. At national level, a network of laws ensures our security as citizens. We have been given rights which enable us to enjoy our private property and personal freedoms.

At every level there has been a trade-off against us; there are a lot of things we're not allowed to do. We can't drive over a certain speed, or strike another person or take somebody else's property. We have to submit to countless of our nation's rules in order to be secure and enjoy our lives. These rules are like a castle, protecting us in the war of all against all.

The 'war' goes on outside this network of changing rules, but the rules themselves are based on something for something. We have a freedom or benefit by allowing others a freedom or benefit. We survive by allowing others to survive.

Moral rules support our survival

We sometimes think of moral rules as having a hallowed origin, as evidencing the nobility of the human being, but their origin appears to be rather more prosaic; they are servants of the survival process. They provide the preconditions of community life. We have to be able to turn our back on our fellows, knowing that our life and property are secure. Hence there must be rules in some form which forbid physical violence, theft and sexual harm. Without them, the community would become anarchic and die. The refinement and evolution of such rules is a practical matter. Even two primitive hunters in the jungle need an understanding about how they are to behave toward each other, if they are to have the advantage of working together.

Moral rules may modify and regulate our behaviour, but like laws they also regulate the behaviour of our fellow-citizens; they provide us with security, and promote our survival. It's the quid pro quo of community life.

We give something for something - up to a point

The utopian idea of a free, fair and equal society is one which some biologists argue is not achievable because of the competitive nature of the gene pool. It seems obvious that even if a fair and equal division of resources could be achieved, some people or groups would do better than others, and inequalities would soon emerge. Sharing the benefits of the planet with perceived equity may have a lot to do with attaining political stability, but the obvious evidence of the human condition is that we move to share social benefits in a niggardly, reactive way.

As individuals, we appear to only give up so much of our advantage in any situation as is necessary to protect our concept of ourselves and our view of our entitlement. This thought seems to apply as much to the attitude of the community in which we live, and the state, as it does to us personally. Advancement of self interest is the obvious objective in negotiations between local and national authorities. Is it surprising? If, to assuage the disadvantage of others, we were required to give up our home or our savings, or the local park, or part of the territory of our nation, our instincts would reject such a move.

Why should we bother to be kind?

If we are driven by the self-interested nature of our survival impulse, why should we bother to be kind at all? Why not just slog it out in an *almost* dog-eat-dog world? One possible answer is that kindness tends to create a more pleasant environment for us. And pleasure remains one of those elements of our wanting nature and of happiness.

Kindness is double-edged. We get the benefit of a sunny environment created by our kindness, and so does the person who receives our kindness. If we are kind to somebody, the chances are that they will reciprocate. If we show compassion and generosity of heart to those around us, we create a benevolent environment for ourselves. Good things for us can flow from this enlightened self-interest.

If, as a result of our coldness, lack of interest, lack of feeling or our aggressive attitudes, a personal relationship or our environment is blighted, it's not to our advantage. An unfavourable climate is created. It's against our interests.

Are we actually altruistic?

Can we go as far as to say that we can act with regard for others rather than ourselves? Many parents will have put their children first and disregarded themselves, but how more generally altruistic we are is a question which is very difficult to answer categorically.

Our self-interested nature hardly allows altruism, although the outcome of a particular act of ours may sometimes *appear* to be based on regard for the other person rather than ourselves. What seems to be altruism can at times be a form of enlightened self interest. We're treating others as we would have them treat us.

A person who picks up his picnic garbage when he is walking in the countryside, even though nobody is watching, may be doing so because he expects other people to leave a clean walk for him. This is not really altruism.

What looks like altruism can also be the result of cultural conditioning – 'women and children first' – or giving up a seat in a crowded train to an old person.

What about those who are trained to risk their lives to save ours – the firemen, beach-guards, air and sea rescue workers, or soldiers? They are conditioned to take risks most of us couldn't face. Their work nevertheless demands a high level of commitment to the lives and safety of other people which in many cases we do identify as altruism.

Altruism is thus difficult to identify in practice. We cannot say whether people are naturally or inherently altruistic. What we can see is, that beyond duty, beyond conditioning, beyond religious sacrifice, there appears to be a thread of respect for the life of others and disregard of self which we can sometimes identify as personal altruism.

Arguably, it appears in a social form in communities which have turned away from the death penalty, or those which accept the social responsibility of caring for the gravely disabled – both of these practices at high cost without any kind of 'return' to the taxpayer.

It's the antithesis of self-interest where a person risks his own life for another, and at the same time, an extreme example of respect for life, and an assertion of the primacy of survival. But it is a rare flower.

Conclusion

There does not seem to be any reason to believe that we are any less selfish and self-interested than our forbears were, but we are much more civilised. If we were not selfish and self-interested, if we did not want insatiably, the force that drives us would be gone.

Our selfishness is modified at a personal level by understanding that the effect created by kindness, compassion and generosity toward others is not only necessary for our more effective survival, but is part of the environment of peace which is essential for our happiness.

Chapter 3

TOLERATING UNPREDICTABILITY

We can be happy if we understand and accept that change and unpredictability are at the core of our existence and constantly affect our lives. An attitude of tolerance of unpredictability is essential for an environment of calm and enjoyment.

Existence, a process of constant change

We can see people in other countries suffering vast changes through wars, famines and natural disasters, but change is everywhere. Change, sometimes almost imperceptible, affects each of us personally in every minute of every day.

In complete contrast, we tend to think of our existence as solid, permanent, and repetitive. This thought is assisted by having all sorts of services on call, like doctors, supermarkets, firemen and hospitals. We press a button and it happens, petrol at the pump and cash at the bank. Our existence therefore appears to have *some* of the qualities of permanence. This is a comforting illusion.

Striving to maintain the status quo

What is more, we strive to keep today the same as yesterday because we think it's more likely to deliver what we want. We like predictability and sameness; we've retained the old Latin word, *status quo*, as a description. With our watches on our wrists, we live and work to time. We anticipate that the television is going to screen our preferred news programme on schedule. We set up little routines, a meal at a certain time, a game of cards with friends on Saturday afternoon, a visit to Grandpa on Sunday. Our household habits, working day, and vacations, often depend on sameness, on predictability, and we find this soothing.

We probably all know a family who go to Skegness or Bournemouth on their annual holiday *every* year; they love these places because they can predict that they will have an enjoyable time. A vacation in a new place can be surprising; it takes a bit of getting used to, and there's a risk that it will fall short of the pleasure we've come to expect. So Skegness; it's more of the same. We're wedded to the status quo.

The inertia of the status quo

Wanting to carry on the same routine of living is by no means limited to our personal habits. As any politician or community worker who wants to implement changes knows, the vested interests of all sorts of groups in society will try to resist change.

Reform of the civil service, local government, health services, schools and political institutions like the British House of Lords attract opponents from all ideologies however inefficient, costly or even unfair the present services may be. Inertia grips society 'as it is' making change difficult, slow, and sometimes virtually impossible in the period of years available to a political party.

The levers to accomplish change exist in a democratic society, but they are not easy to work in a progressive way.

However, despite human inclinations, change cannot be arrested.

We know that everything is changing all the time

It's startling if we suddenly bring to mind that *everything is changing all the time* – us, other people, the earth and all the things on it. We know this is true, but we don't always focus on its implications. We want our existence to be secure and predictable. We look at ourselves more closely, and see we too are changing like the leaves on the trees, or the animals in the fields, growing in experience but unfortunately, ageing.

Scientists tell us that everything in the universe, including us, is made up of *moving* energy particles which give the illusion of solidity. Consider our planet, hurtling through space, suffering volcanic eruptions, the extinction of species of animals, and climate change, and all the time flexing its tectonic plates to try to shake down those earthquake-proof buildings in Tokyo.

Natural forces are only part of the spectrum of change and unpredictability. Wars and revolutions threaten and happen. Our free market economic system, prized as the key to prosperity, collapses. The bank failures and tsunamis come when they come. It's the process of existence moving remorselessly on.

The change process makes life unpredictable

As individuals, we really don't have very much control over the events happening to us, or around us, despite our conviction that the light in the kitchen will go on when we flick the switch. Change is obviously so significant because it makes our lives uncertain and unpredictable. We don't know whether tomorrow we're going to have a doctor with an X ray in his hand frown at us and say he has some bad news. A car accident, a fire, a robbery, a war, each can tear our life apart. A decision by the management at our work could change the shape of our life overnight. We can scarcely live without the electricity which powers all the appliances in our home, and yet it can fail.

Of course, so many parts of our support system don't fail (but they will certainly change), and many happy constructive changes happen too. But the whole point is that life's unpredictable, *and this unpredictability* is a crucial element in the anxieties of everyday life. To be happy we have to have a way of dealing with it.

The unpredictability of small events

We tend to associate unpredictability with the big life and death issues, without realising how it also affects all the small things that make up the day and are vital for our good humour and ease. Finding there's no coffee left in the jar; wondering whether our child will score in the football game; worrying about how serious the leak in the roof is; and whether there's time to walk to the train; thinking that the visit to the dentist is going to be painful, or hoping that our friend will not be late, as he usually is, for the meeting at the pub. So many small events in the day have an element of uncertainty and unpredictability.

Often circumstances around those events, about which we know nothing, are having their effect too. The taxi is late because the telephone operator was confused by another call. The chairman of the meeting is irritable because he had an argument with his wife. Who knows why the attendance at the village fair was so poor this year? Or why the central heating boiler failed in the cold snap? Or why the traffic was so heavy on a normally clear road when we were in a hurry? There are probably quite rational answers to these events, but we will never know them.

We react to not getting what we expect

We've been on vacation, and our flight is delayed at the airport; hours of sitting around! Or we go on a picnic, and we've just laid out the sandwiches on the rug when the dog gets his paws in the salad! This is where we get the feeling that things just don't work out the way we want. It's that very feeling of dissatisfaction which makes us *react*. More often than not, we find a way around our little difficulty. We have a latte and a cake and endure the airport delays; we throw away the picnic salad and say we have plenty of food anyway. That's why we're survivors. The state of mind that enables us to do this calmly is an essential part of happiness.

The unpredictability of people

And, if we want to bring change and the uncertainty it causes to a very human point, why wasn't our nomination accepted for that vacancy on the committee? One can never tell what human beings are going to do when they have to make decisions, let alone the management at work! Virtually any decision which has to be made by a group of people is relatively uncertain, and sometimes astounding, whether it be at the factory, the office, the club, the residents' association or in the courts. This is not to mention decisions made by political parties! We react to these unsatisfactory events every day. We find a way through them. We're survivors. *But we suffer more anxiety and tension than necessary,* unless we have a tolerance of unpredictability.

The unpredictability of everything

If we step back a bit, we can see that the picture of the earth and the human beings on it, is one of continual and often cataclysmic change, whether we're thinking about ourselves personally, our activities as human-kind, or the geographical crust of the planet and the universe. We actually live, every minute of every day, with the uncertainty that change produces. The *appearance* of solidity and predictability seems to be no more than an appearance. And we have to accept that we are part of this inexorable process of change. If we think of ourselves as infinitesimal parts of a process of change, our personal anxieties seem rather small.

Do we have to go with the flow?

The old saying of the sixties, *go with the flow,* quite sensibly suggested that we should relax when confronted by the unexpected, and accept what we can't change. The saying conjures up a river, with us on the bank, deciding whether to step in. It implies that we don't have to go with the flow if we don't want to. We should be able to see that we don't have any options here. *The river doesn't have any banks.* There's nowhere to stand still and keep our feet dry.

We're in it, whether we like it or not. Sure, we can oppose change; we can fight it, just as we could swim against the current for a while; but we have to suffer its impact. We have to *deal* with this process of change and uncertainty, every time we are affected, by finding another way. This is the challenge, and the reason we keep moving relentlessly on.

Living with conflict

Solving the problem of not getting what we want and expect creates conflict. It is often conflict with other people, but it may be conflict with circumstances, like a flood, or a fall in the stock market. We always have the option to accept the situation and not oppose. Acceptance is discussed more fully in Chapter 4.

A more common reaction to conflict is to face it. Our instincts make us react to conflict by solving, or trying to solve, the problems caused by unpredictable events, whether it's a big event like loss of our job, or a small event like how to stop the noise of our car alarm. Because we rarely sit back and ignore events we don't like, we're often in conflict. Conflict means more than just arguing with somebody; it includes struggling with circumstances that are working against us (like an unobtainable telephone number that we need urgently, or that unstoppable car alarm!).

Yes, there are those moments where we are doing something pleasant like watching a movie, eating a delicious meal, or having a glass of wine with friends. But in the background there will usually be a chain of conflict issues, like the dispute we are having with the plumber about his charges, a problem with the tax office, or the headache getting the new software on our computer to work properly. Much of the time we're facing the issues caused by the difference between what *we want* and what *we get;* and what we get is what is delivered by the process of change.

Trying to dodge conflict

We know that unless conflicts can be faced forthrightly and resolved, they are destructive at both a personal and a social level. This fear of destructive effects tends to drive us all into denial. Conflict is the same whether we view it personally or as a member of a group, a community, a culture, or a nation.

We usually look on conflict as undesirable, difficult and depressing, and in many ways it can be. We identify sound leadership with avoidance of conflict. It seems to be accepted that the hallmark of a good company manager is one who runs a 'smooth operation' free of friction. As a parent, we sometimes try to persuade our children to believe that life ought to be without frustration. We know that religious systems aim for bliss; utopian communes claim to be without grudges and grievances. And in our communities we have people of high status to banish conflict on our behalf; judges, politicians, priests, and psychiatrists.

But of course, despite this aversion from conflict, we live in it like fishes in water. We can only avoid conflict by having a dreamless sleep, meditating, indulging in sensual pleasure, or being absorbed in a personal task, but these are short term options. Life seems to be conflict. Even if a person lived alone in a cave, there would be a difference between what he wanted and what he got; withdrawal to a small closed community of the like-minded could bring its conflicts too. There really doesn't appear to be any way for us to avoid that struggle against people or circumstances which seem to be against us.

Despite our tendency to go into denial about conflict, resolving it effectively is actually what makes us survivors. Conflict is an every-day, every-moment problem, and it's right to remember, therefore, that at a personal level it is not something exceptional or unlucky. Every conflict involves a challenge to which we respond, searching for a solution.

Unsatisfied wanting drives us

Our dynamics appear to work like this: we cannot satisfy our wants completely and perfectly because existence is an unpredictable process of change. Hence we have tensions and anxieties. We react to the unsatisfactory result of not getting precisely what we want, and the conflict it creates, by solving the problem – trying to satisfy our want another way.

Of course, that new solution may not produce precisely what we want either (more worries), but it will often be an advance. We don't rest there. As a result of the new situation, we develop new wants and expectations. Again, they may be defeated or fall short. We are challenged to find yet another solution, and we do.

We go on and on in this problem-solving way, driven by our unsatisfied wants, always having to deal with the tensions and anxieties that they create in an unpredictable world.

This doesn't mean that we *never* get what we want. On a lot of occasions we do. It means that the general tenor of our life is that we are continually challenged by not getting what we want, and we are continually responding.

What can we do to approach happiness?

We have to accept reality and realise that not-getting-what-we-want is the challenge. We know that the difference between what we want, and what we get, is simply the way things are. Reality. We often *have* to suffer the anxiety of wanting something and the disappointment of not getting it. But we can see that this quality of life which causes our anxieties, this 'unsatisfactoriness', is far from being a reason for gloom and despondency; it is the challenge which drives us on.

If we understand the unpredictability process, we can get events into proportion more easily. Understanding the normality and dynamics of the unpredictability process acts like a stabiliser on an ocean liner in rough seas. We tolerate change and the unpredictability it generates instead of being upset by it. Toleration of unpredictability becomes part of our approach to problems, part of our waking life. It doesn't mean that we don't feel anxiety and concern; it's just that we can cope with it more easily.

A *key factor in moving toward an environment of enjoyment is making sure our wants are proportionate to the event. We have to examine and re-examine what we are asking in all things.* Of course this isn't easy. If we ask ourselves whether we've pitched our wants and expectations too high on a specific occasion, in many cases we'll probably find that we have. And we can make the necessary adjustment. That will be a relief. We will be wanting less, and very much more at ease.

* Chapter 4 *

HOW CAN WE ACCEPT THE WAY IT IS?

Acceptance and detachment are positive attitudes which we can cultivate to work broadly in our lives; a mental environment of peace and enjoyment cannot be created without them.

Acceptance can be used to reduce our tensions and anxieties. It involves acceptance of the unpredictability of our lives, as outlined in the previous chapter, and, more generally, acceptance of the ways that we can be deceived by our self-image. It can give insight into the need to question who we think we are, refocus, and reconcile with the way things are.

We know we can't opt out of the conflicts of every day and live in a sunny glade with an ever-present smile on our faces. We may have lots of pleasures, but there are anxieties too, and we have to face them.

Two roads

Usually there are two roads open for us to deal with the conflicts of daily life. One is or can be anger-related; the other has a measure of acceptance and detachment. We have the option which way to go. Of course it's not always a considered option. Sometimes we're rushed by our emotions along an anger-related path.

We can't accept *everything* that happens to us and nor should we. If we can change a situation to our way, we will – that may involve the conflicts described in the last chapter. There can't be anything wrong with that. But even that course will be assisted if we travel along with a spirit of acceptance.

But how do we treat the things that happen to us that we *can't* change to our way, the things that we're forced to accept – the hard realities around us?

Anger-related feelings – our default setting

The word 'anger' is here used as a key word for anger-related feelings; included are all those miserable feelings we have occasionally, ranging from disaffection, irritation and intolerance, right up to malice, loathing, outright hatred and potential aggression.

Anger in the broad sense as defined, seems to be our default setting, our instinctive reaction to certain problems. In extreme cases, in a violent society, it's apparent that anger can operate as a survival mechanism, energizing a person to react when he might need to protect himself. But today we can't punch somebody on the nose because he stands on our toe, even though we might feel like it, unless we want a whole lot more trouble with the police.

Anger as a warning

We live in a community where, for the most part, dispute resolution is the task of the police and the judiciary. Anger, as a survival reaction for us, is simply inappropriate in ninety-nine point nine per cent of cases. Does anger have any other function which might be helpful? Over the whole range of our personal problems anger, that instinctive emotional reaction, can act as a warning. We can imagine it as a red light flashing. The red light can spur us to think, 'Wait, what's happening here?' It can actually give us an opportunity for a cooler appraisal.

The anger virus

The first thing we notice about our anger is that it's *ours*. It's like a virus or fever inside us; it can make us feel sick; it can blight our enjoyment. At times anger can be disabling; our veins seem to fill with poison. At the lesser end of the scale, irritation and intolerance can cast a grey cloud of depression over us. This is a virus which it seems sensible to avoid.

Some psychologists may say that anger is a release, and even energizing. It's certainly a natural reaction. It ought to be recognised, not stifled. It can be used as a pointer to another way, but it's not necessarily uplifting or helpful to an ordinary person in his day to day experiences.

Anger as a tool

Our experience tends to show us that anger isn't very effective as a tool to solve a problem. There may have been occasions when we've displayed our temper, and somebody has backed down, but it doesn't happen very often that way. We may have had the experience as parents of shouting at our kids when they were small, and not getting very far; we may have become more angry at being so impotent. A person blows his top with the post office clerk – and is ignored. If somebody treats us badly, flaring up doesn't help – a waiter in a restaurant offers a person a table next to the lavatory, a vendor in the market drops some rotten fruit into his bag, a cab-driver tries on a blatant over-charge. These things are happening to everybody, all the time. We haven't been singled out. To get the results we want in the restaurant, the market, or on a cab-ride we have hopefully learned that it can pay to take a gentler line.

Another point about anger which can be very nasty is that it sometimes causes anger in the person we're abusing; a shouting match ensues in which we make our position worse. Even the waiter, eyeing an almost empty restaurant can say, 'Sorry, all our other tables are reserved.'

Anger can erode our judgment

Anger can make a person less, not more, competent to handle a difficulty. We've seen somebody fly off the handle with a salesgirl, or a friend, only to find afterwards that they've got the facts all wrong. They often regret the outburst and say, 'If only I had kept my cool...' or, 'If only I'd thought about it first...'

Anger makes us look foolish

There's nothing very uplifting in anger. A person can look as though he's lost control, not only of himself, but of the situation he's in, and often he has. Afterwards, he may realise that his anger is related to his sense of who he is, and his sense of who he is, is usually askew.

We think when we get angry, 'How can anybody have the nerve to treat *me* like this?' or, '*I'm* entitled to better than this', or, 'This is grossly unfair to *me*'. If we consider these thoughts, all based on *I, me, what I want, what I deserve,* and *what I'm entitled to,* in relation to who we really are, we'll often remember that we don't own the airline, the shop or the restaurant; and we don't have a claim much different to anybody else's; we're just a passenger, or a customer. We have to sit in line at the medical centre because we're just another patient; no more or less important than the others. We have probably seen that anger in the family can be widely hurtful because it pollutes the atmosphere, and in the end, we may not be able to control or direct the family member who has got under our skin.

But we're entitled to be angry!

People feel the dark emotions here mentioned every week. The question is whether they're going to go on in the default mode, or try something else. At times when somebody has suffered a wrong we've heard them say, 'I feel very, very angry. And I'm entitled to feel angry because…' What they are really saying is that they are entitled to take on the misery of anger. Sure, they are, but then the light may dawn – this so-called right is a self-inflicted injury on top of the trouble they already have.

It all starts with us

We've found that the world isn't going to move over and make a nice space for us, unfortunately. We can work, study, have a family, build a business or even start a political movement; but even in the framework of the change that we bring about ourselves, there will be so much that we don't agree with, and we dislike, hence tension, stress, anxiety. Anger related feelings are always stirring. If we can't do much about what's going on 'out there' at least we can examine our own attitude toward it.

Whose problem is it anyway?

When a person can blame somebody else for his problem, or his worry, he tends to do so. He starts generating the anger-related feelings, and perhaps actions. The event which caused the anger has happened, but the reaction, the anger, is his.

The solution to his conflict is in him. He has to accept facts; they've happened. It doesn't mean the other person who may have caused the problem is innocent. It just means that the 'wounded' person has the option not to focus on the perpetrator in a vengeful way. He may then see that avoiding anger is an advantage to him.

We can reach within ourselves, and choose to treat the conflicting action of another person as a natural force, like a gale or an icy shower or a bolt of lightning. It's what happens on our journey every day, and there's no point in us getting angry with a gale, an icy shower or a bolt of lightning.

Anger and relationships with other people

It's possible to look at a relationship with another person as being like a separate living thing of which we are part; it's fragile and it needs tender care. Every time a person metaphorically kicks a relationship because he's in a bad temper, he can leave a bruise which may not quite heal. The more bruises, the less likely the healing. We know from experience that relationships can only take so much kicking before they fall apart, and we have to be aware that we may be the one who pays the penalty for that –

the penalty of loss. It's unpleasant and it doesn't make much sense to have relationships which limp along sadly before falling apart, but this is what can happen on the anger road.

Understanding and accepting the quality of life

At the lower end of the anger spectrum is the irritation, stress and anxiety of an ordinary day. This pressure is constant, and continuous. Of course we may have many good days, but at the same time, we also have to cope with an undercurrent of unsatisfactoriness. Telephone lines are engaged, buses are late, people uncooperative, and the engineer doesn't arrive when he promised to fix the central heating. This situation is *the way things are*, for everybody – all the time. Yes, we hopefully have a lot of good days, but sometimes a whole sequence of events seem to go against us, trouble with our health, with our friends, with our work, with our income tax. People make promises to us that they don't live up to.

We know that we're not the sole target of chance. We're not a victim. Just being conscious means that everybody has to deal with this unsatisfactory state. We can have the insight that our expectations are not in general going to be met precisely, or at all in some cases; but we keep on striving. When we *accept* that this is the way life is, it's easier to cope.

This understanding of the quality of life is the first aspect of acceptance. Our mental picture of our environment of peace and enjoyment will necessarily include this undercurrent of unsatisfactoriness. Our attitude of acceptance and detachment neutralises it and enables us to cope with it. This doesn't diminish our enjoyment. We could say that unsatisfactoriness is part of the wallpaper in our mental environment. This is not pessimism; it's realism.

Is life really this sort of suffering?

There is an ancient adage that 'life is suffering, and suffering is caused by desire'. This is quite a profound psychological observation, but we need to interpret it to relate to our life. Most of us don't suffer personally, although many people on the planet do. We rather share lives which have an undercurrent of the 'unsatisfactory'. We endure the anxiety, the tension, the stress. Nor do we desire in a raging, fiery sense. We merely want something or somebody at different intensities of desire all the time. But the conclusion is the same. With all our wants and disappointments come tension, anxiety, stress – and sometimes, pain.

Would an end of desire stop suffering?

If life has an element of the unsatisfactory, and this feeling is caused by wanting, will the unsatisfactoriness cease if we stop wanting? Logically, yes. This is what motivates the people who have sought happiness by giving away their possessions, or putting themselves into a trance-like state. But a complete end of desire or wanting would be death, or a continuous mindless trance where we ceased to be affected by the constant change going on around us – a state so near death it could not be described as life.

But none of these approaches to the anxieties generated

by our wants will be acceptable to most of us. As suggested, wanting to live is at the root of our impulses, and all our other wants flow from that. For most of us it's inescapable that, as long as we're alive and have the will to live, we'll be wanting.

What is, however, instructive about the adage, and evident, is that there is a relationship between the scale of our wants and the extent of our anxiety. Big, unrealistic wants bring big anxiety and disappointment. Small wants, small anxiety.

Acceptance and enjoyment

In the dictionary, acceptance is simply consent to receive something. There is a wider concept; it is *seeking to be in harmony with things and people around us;* a life in which we can feel at ease, enjoy and attempt to realise our potential. In this sense I think it is clear that a measure of acceptance can minimize our worries; we are seeking a harmonious environment.

What is enjoyment?

Enjoyment, as defined here, means we have the satisfaction in knowing we are using our time in what is to us the most meaningful way. Enjoyment isn't necessarily a high pressure surge of pleasure. Often, it's a quiet, reflective appreciation of things and people. Part of our enjoyment may even be to understand objectively the constant conflict between what we want, and the facts as they really are. We can work out what can't be changed – often a difficult task – and what has to be accepted. And then we can pursue detachment.

Pretended acceptance

It's obvious that keeping quiet about a difficulty isn't acceptance. If a person grits his teeth, and gets churned up inside, but doesn't show an outward sign about a situation he dislikes – that's not acceptance, although it may look like it to those around him. He would still carry the emotional burden and suffering of the event. Acceptance involves seeking to be genuinely at ease in all our important actions and relationships, at work, and with friends and family.

It seems to follow that we can only achieve harmony out of conflict, when we accept what change has unpredictably delivered to us, unless of course it's a situation we can change, and want to change.

Acceptance doesn't mean backing down

Acceptance can't mean approving things we disapprove of, or not taking action to change situations which we can, and ought to change. But an *attitude* of acceptance and detachment can assist us, and reduce our anxiety, even in the most fiery conflict.

We can look at acceptance as a damage limitation exercise. If *we* can't change what has happened, we have to deal with the reality. And the reality is us. We *can* modify our self-image; who we think we are. We can modify what we want. It seems sensible to deal with that reality in the way that hurts us least, the way that minimizes our anxiety.

How do we decide what can't be changed?

Sometimes it may be easy to decide what we have to

accept because it's obvious; for example if we worked for a company that went broke, we couldn't do anything about that in itself. But often, deciding what we *have* to accept is a complex problem. Many, perhaps most of the conflicts we have, arise from a situation which presents us with options. Suppose a person has a boundary dispute with his neighbour. Should he go and talk to the neighbour for the third time, or sue him? Suppose he and his girlfriend disagree whether to have a baby. Should he sever the relationship, or accept her view? Is the issue really a make or break one? These, and a thousand more problems like them, can confront us every day. And there is no magic answer. We will be on the edge of the stress of conflict, and the peace of acceptance all the time.

Coping with the loss of somebody dear

There are cases where events have occurred which we find deeply upsetting, but *have* to accept, like illness, or loss of life.

The loss of a loved one is very hard to accept. Grief and mourning are natural, and have to be allowed their time; but there is a point where grief is not about the loved one, but about us. We're sorry for ourselves. We want our loved one near us, and the unpredictable course of events has taken him or her away.

We suffer the pain that comes from that conflict between what we *want,* and what life has actually delivered.

We have to go through the same thought process here, as we do with the simple everyday frustration of unpredictable events. We have to try to recognise how much the 'I want' factor, our self-image, is involved. Our expectations have been defeated. Are we going to ask for what we can't possibly have?

Being conscious of this process may make recovery from our loss easier. We will be living in the present, not trying impossibly to live in the past, or in a dream-land of what might have been.

Grief is like a burden, and it makes sense to discard it as soon as we can. Living is now. There's a line in a poem by Homer where some soldiers, tired from fighting, come upon the bodies of their dead compatriots on the battlefield at the end of the day. Homer says, 'First they ate, and then they wept.' We can't be as matter-of-fact as those ancient soldiers, but we can try to be realistic about grief.

What if somebody causes us grave loss?

When we're a victim, it's hard for us not to hate our aggressor. If we were seriously injured in a hit and run accident, or if, say, our child was murdered, our instinctive reaction would probably be to hate, and want revenge upon the perpetrator. There are cases where victims of crime go on year after year hating the perpetrator, seeking what they call 'justice' or 'closure.' We can see the suffering in their faces because these cases are often well publicised on television. The victims sometimes vow that their life is ruined, and, in truth, it may be. The hatred such victims feel must be like a painful cancer. It only takes a moment's reflection to think that we wouldn't want that cancer making us ache on top of the hurt we had already suffered.

But this is surely the hardest loss to cope with. We can

lose money, friends, and jobs, and these events are at least manageable by us; we can do something about them. But to be a victim of serious crime would be shocking, whether it happened to us or to somebody very close to us. The pain of this would be ours, it would come initially from the shock of the event, and later from our anger, and desire for revenge.

It's not strictly true to say of the perpetrator, as many victims do, 'He ruined my life.' Yes, he caused the tragedy in the first place, but the real pain is in our anger, and unsatisfied desire for revenge. It's against common sense for us to carry the burden of hatred too far, and this insight may make it easier for us to shed it.

Sometimes we are able to personalise hatred

Personalising hatred can extend from serious crimes to trivial arguments. If we can identify the person who harmed us, our anger is so much more potent – somebody jostles a person in the street and he flares up. A kid daubs paint on a neighbour's fence, and he declares he'll wring the kid's neck. A shop assistant is rude to a customer, who then shouts for the manager. A car cuts sharply in front of ours, and our temperature goes up! This is a stony path, and one it doesn't seem sensible to tread.

The odds are that we are going to get buffeted about in this flow of change. The fact that we can sometimes identify the person who caused our distress, recognise him as a living human being, is a great temptation for us to focus anger upon him – at our own cost in additional misery. It can be better to regard him as one of those natural forces that sometimes hurt us, like a storm; if we do, it's easier for us. We wouldn't hate an avalanche which injured our daughter while she was skiing, or a wave that drowned her while surfing. We'd grieve for her, but we'd be free of the legacy of hate which can be aroused when another identifiable human being is the cause.

We have the option of trying to treat these unpredictable human offences which hurt us as natural forces; it's just bad luck in a world which is ever-changing, day by day, hour by hour.

Our attachment to people and property

Detachment appears to be a necessary part of acceptance. We haven't accepted a situation if we haven't let it go, and moved on. We have to detach ourselves. The chosen definition of detachment is simply *not being attached to something or someone* (and not some kind of other-worldly detachment as in a dream or trance). Attachment, the opposite of detachment, is an expression of 'I want!'

In considering detachment, it's helpful to recognise our attachments first. We're attached to ideas, memories, institutions, personal loyalties, money, property, our family and friends. We're attached also in a more subtle way to our culture. We 'want' all these things and people; they are part of the furniture of our life. If anybody tried to prise them away from us, we would almost certainly react with dismay, and other strong emotions. In a different sense, we're also attached in a habitual and uncritical way to certain emotional states, particularly, as suggested, our default setting of anger. On the instant, anger can seem to be the way.

Attachment implies possession, ownership, or control of somebody or something. It's part of the 'I want' side of us, part of our self-image; it's what we think we're entitled to. Our view of ourselves, because it's likely to be inaccurate, can prevent us from getting any clear vision of our attachments. We can easily identify the attachment as such – our car, our farm etc. What we have difficulty with is our emotional attitude toward our car or our farm.

Our attachments in human relationships appear to be complex emotionally, far beyond our faulty vision. How much are we attached to our father, mother, or our child? And how much are they attached to us? We don't necessarily *feel* the same about each other. These attachments aren't measurable; they are complex beyond our understanding.

Our attachments can't be absolute

It's true that laws, civil contracts, moral rules, culture and customs give us rights or customs of possession, ownership and control over people and property. We have our children, our land, our partner, our citizenship. But we know that circumstances can affect these rights – war, political reform, civil disorder, revolution, sudden death, cultural change, and changes of heart in people.

Nothing in our society is set in stone. So while a person may have, say, a piece of paper which records that he is entitled to an acre of land, or a bank deposit, there is a certain point beyond which he can't own or control them. The land is taken by decree; the bank fails. Civil contracts, promises, and marriages can all be broken.

If we think of an attachment between adult people, like marriage, partnership, or friendship, when the other party acts to end it, there is little we can do but pick up the pieces.

The problem is that when attachments relate to us, we see them first through the tunnel-vision of self-image – *my* home, *my* child, *my* share portfolio. It's hard to have any real perspective and balance in viewing our attachments. It's possible to let go to a degree, and achieve a measure of detachment, if we view them understanding that our vision of ourselves is likely to be faulty. It's our view of ourselves which causes our sense of loss, our frustration and pain, when we are deprived of something or someone we're attached to.

Can we step back and take a cooler, longer view? Can we, as it were, extract our emotional self from the problem? The factors which have forced us to consider our attachment are often beyond our control – a bankruptcy, a flood, a new law. And they can even be beyond our full comprehension – a change in the attitude of a friend or a partner, a difference that we didn't see coming.

Change often erodes or sweeps away our precious attachments; adjustments are likely to be forced upon us. If a person can develop a sense of detachment, he won't get hung up about something he can't change, or perhaps fully understand. He can then see that if he lets go, he will break the painful bond of attachment. Letting go involves moving on to a new 'now,' with a real feeling that the problem doesn't raise his emotional temperature any longer; it's part of the past.

Giving and detachment

Thinking about giving can help with detachment, because in becoming detached from a problem, in a sense we're giving it away. Giving and detachment are the same in this context. If a person gives something when feeling disgruntled, deprived or reluctant, be it a cheque to a charity, or a book to a friend, he's still attached to it; he hasn't really 'given' it in his heart. If he gives what he doesn't need, like old clothes to a jumble sale, he's not giving at all; he's disposing of junk. If he can give something which is, or might have been, significant to him, and feel free of it, then he can get the feeling that the strings of attachment have snapped. Feeling detached from a difficulty is a good feeling.

When something upsetting happens, it's often a good idea to try to walk on. Just as we would avoid stepping on a dog's mess in the street, we can have a sense that we can step over our troubles and dismiss them from our thoughts; accept the happening, and become detached. And then get on with the very important business of enjoying life!

Conclusion

Acceptance and detachment are simple concepts, but difficult to achieve as an attitude in practice. They don't mean that we should submit to everything. They don't have to inhibit us from engaging in the conflicts of everyday living. They make it easier for us to cope with the ups and down of life.

Acceptance and detachment don't just happen. They need to be cultivated as an attitude to life. They need to be kept in mind in the daily march. If we can do this we can create an environment of peace and enjoyment, both in our mind and externally. We need to ask in a hundred situations, 'Is there a need for acceptance and detachment here?'

Chapter 5

WHAT DOES IT ALL MEAN?

One crucial element of happiness is the belief that we are engaged in life in a way which we regard as meaningful.

Meaning in a personal sense, and the meaning of life

The search for meaning – we want to know things, because we survive more effectively by knowing. There is our own personal enquiry in the minutiae of our lives, and there is the vast quest for meaning in many forms of science, some of which we learn about, much of which we are not capable of understanding.

A huge amount of scientific effort has been devoted to finding out what's going on in the cosmos; but wanting to know, wanting to understand the meaning of a situation is the province of everybody. On a personal level, we want to make sense of something, whether it's a road map or why our computer misbehaves, or why we're on the planet. We search to understand, and if we can, we can either be comfortable, or know the disadvantage we're facing.

What has meaning got to do with our happiness?

Giving our lives meaning is fundamental to happiness. There can be no environment for enjoyment unless it has meaning for us. We might live in a place which is barren in a physical sense, bare mountains and desert, yet have a meaningful life there. But in any environment, whatever its material comforts, where negative doctrines prevail, where beliefs are rejected, where everything is thought to be pointless, where scepticism effectively denies our existence, there can be no enjoyment – only depression and despair. In such a place, we would be living in the shadow of a nihilistic death-wish, which is the antithesis of our natural will to survive and prosper.

But this nihilism is a summation of life which only a few extreme individuals make; few of us will come close to it. The search for meaning is a natural part of our 'wants' and is implicit in our will to survive. The discovery of meaning is something which happens to us in small ways every day. We go on beyond these discoveries, as individuals and communities, always searching.

In a quest for meaning it's helpful to start by looking at the big framework of our existence.

Scientific understanding

Scientists haven't yet been able to tell us what the meaning of life is, or whether there is a meaning, despite the huge progress they have made toward understanding the cosmos. The physicist Richard Feynman said that there were many things he didn't know, and that he wasn't absolutely sure of anything very much in the scientific sense. Many scientists share this view. A lot of very advanced science is about a territory of possible answers, and degrees of certainty. But the scientific search for meaning goes on, and will go on as long as we survive; it's a natural, elemental and thrilling drive.

Religious understanding

Whether we can believe that there is a spiritual ordering of the universe is a difficult question. Many people cannot find sufficient evidence to become convinced that there is a spiritual order in what are actually human testimonies and man-made institutions. But there is no doubt that religious and mystical belief has been, and still is, a survival tool for many people.

It is very difficult for some people to accept that we are alone and responsible for ourselves. If a person places the cause of events outside himself, believing that he is in the hands of a supreme being, he seems to have a more comfortable position. Events, even dire events, become 'God's will'. He seems to have moved a weight of responsibility off his own shoulders – *but not completely*, because to get this 'benefit,' he has to decide that he has faith. It's a decision for which he is responsible.

Many people cannot accept that there can be a personal God, one who cares for us personally, who at the same time allows millions of children to suffer from disease and starvation and die in civil wars, tsunamis and earthquakes. If God is omnipotent, they ask, how can he allow the massive and continuing torture of innocents? If he is not omnipotent, is there any point in regarding him as more than an arbitrary and dangerous force?

Cosmic meaning

Thus the idea of cosmic meaning, whether scientific or religious, is something which, for many people, is simply under review, while others rely upon their religion. This is the preferred way to put the question of cosmic meaning here. It seems very extreme to say, 'If you don't believe in God, the cosmos is meaningless.' We are a tiny part of the cosmos, and we are on a journey which may yield all sorts of answers.

The fact that we are alone on our own small planet, as well as being undeniably alone inside our head, *and* we can find no ultimate and over-reaching cosmic meaning, need not be frightening. On the contrary, it should be energising and exciting. We are obviously a very vibrant part of a natural order, which is pressing on relentlessly. The richness, the fascination, and the meaning in our lives can be in our ultimately unknowable relationships with others; in other words, at an earthly rather than a cosmic level.

It may be that mankind's drive for survival itself, the great panoply of change leading to crisis and struggle which we see around us every day, this amazing journey, should be our focus and inspiration. We could then feel fairly relaxed about cosmic meaning, and all the unanswered questions – and await answers with interest!

Earthly meaning

Our real scope is to examine earth-based meaning. Modern life in developed countries presents us with a confusing number of options about how we should live and think. We are less sure of what we should do, or what we want to do. A variety of political philosophies beckon us. The philosophies, like religion, demand levels of acceptance, or leaps of faith, which it is hard to attain. The problem with ideologies and religions is their exclusivity; there is seldom room for other ideas.

If we take a different course, and turn to sensual experience, and the acquisition of possessions as a meaningful goal of life, our lives are cluttered; and we find that houses and cars and vacations do not seem to be enough. Indulgence in sex, drugs and alchohol doesn't seem to be enough either. After initial pleasures, we remain unsatisfied, as we must if we are to go on trying to survive.

Our existence in time

In trying to find meaning in our existence on the planet, we ought to look at it in relation to time, because, whether it is an illusion or not, we appear to live in linear time. We are aware of a hazy past, a chaotic present, and an unknown and uncertain future. And it is self-evident that we are alive now, not yesterday or tomorrow.

Is history meaningless?

When we look back into the past, be it a day ago, a week, or a year, we see our own imperfect mental picture on the screen of our mind. *The past has gone*. Some marks may have been left on the landscape by what happened yesterday, like the shelter in the park which the kids in the street burned down, or the aftermath of a hurricane in Florida. Awful marks may be left on the bodies and minds of people by past strife and death. But the past, good or bad, remains a mental picture for each of us. When we share this experience with other people, it's apparent that their picture may be different, and sometimes very different.

Our picture of the past is also conditioned by the

present; we're far from being dispassionate observers of what happened yesterday.

When the philosopher Karl Popper said that history is meaningless, but we can give it meaning, he meant that everyone sees the past from their own point of view, and they give it meaning by expressing that point of view. If we ask a Russian and a German about the Second World War, we'll get some very different views about causes, as well as differences about what actually happened. An Englishman and an African will have two different pictures of African history. The past is very confused territory; that's why the honest witnesses to a car accident hardly every agree about what happened.

This fact that the past is in the eye of the beholder makes it much easier for us to be aware of the views of others, and, if necessary, it can become a modifying influence upon us before we take a position about a past event.

Being troubled by the past

It's easy to say that we live in the present, and the past doesn't always give a clear picture, but a lot of us are seriously troubled by tragedies in the past. We can think of the bitter and long-time enmities arising from religious and political conflict in Northern Ireland; we think of relations killed in war; and personal problems over the years with relatives who have been seriously ill.

The peace we gain from moving on beyond the past is something we need but find difficult to achieve. It is a start to recognise that it's our state of mind. It's necessary to question our self-image. Have we been conditioned to take a particular view? Can we be sure that our conditioning is exclusively right?

If we dwell on the hurt of the past, it becomes a kind of ache inside us. Can we say, 'I don't want this pain. I'm not going to put up with it any longer'? Can we say, 'The past has happened,' and move into the present? For many of us this will be an aspiration rather than an actuality, but it is a healthy aspiration to have.

Living in the future

We can make plans and have dreams about the future, but they may not happen. Of course plans, hopes and dreams are fine; they can be exciting and absorbing and fun, and they provide a very important basis for future action, but they remain hopes.

Most of us may never have had any expectation of an inheritance, but we can see that waiting for it wouldn't be very smart. We might find that everything had been lost in the stock-market, or more likely that the financial advisers had absorbed all the money in fees. In some cases, living in the future has a tinge of the macabre: 'When Mum dies, we'll have the house.' And we've known of those who have waited in anxiety for years for a specific promotion at the office: 'Everything will come right then,' they say. But nothing is predictable in corporate life except the CEO's bonus, especially when there are management consultants about. Our career may look secure today, and aimed ever upwards, but tomorrow, who can tell?

Living in hopes and dreams doesn't make much sense, but that is not to detract from the motivations and incentives that they provide.

No time for rehearsals

The reality is *this* instant moment when our heart is beating, and we can hopefully see, touch, feel and smell. We sometimes do things half–heartedly, whether it's visiting a new city, listening to a concert, reading a book, or being a friend. And if we're asked why, we usually say that next time it'll be different.

In other words, we often treat now as a rehearsal for next time. Strictly, we know there isn't a next time; now is now, and can never be a rehearsal. Now can never be repeated. Life is a continuous and changing 'reality,' and to appreciate it, we ought to focus on this moment in which we are living.

We have to ask: What's happening? How does it feel? Who and what is around me, and why? What are the people doing? What am I going to make of *this* moment? *Am I enjoying?*

Becoming absorbed in a task shrinks time

A more focussed way of living in the now is when we are absorbed in doing something which interests us. This works well in solitary activity such as reading, writing, sewing, drawing or meditation for example. Our sense of time vanishes or shrinks; we live *in* the task. But this kind of focus can happen at events involving other people, such as listening to a lecture or concert, watching a film, a play – or even attending a committee meeting! And some people, very fortunately, experience absorption in their everyday work.

It's not a bad idea to think about the things that absorb us when we concentrate on them. Activities that absorb us have real meaning and contribute to our happiness.

Getting practice in going slowly

We are always here, where we are at this moment, and it is always now. But we sometimes think, 'I'll just get this done, and then…' In this, too, we are trading the present for the imagined future. We hustle along because it's not now, but the next thing we're interested in. We have a tendency to think that we don't have the time, that time is running against us. Often it's just an illusion.

It is inevitable that we have to hurry at times, and perhaps think only of the meeting we're going to have, or the plane we intend to catch. It's useful to remind ourselves to recognise that, basically, what is important is this moment of our journey, not the arrival, which may never happen, or happen differently than we ever thought it would. We can learn from children in this, as young children generally have no sense of urgency, of the need to get things done. They're usually completely absorbed in now.

If today was our last day

One way to look at living in the moment is to ask this question: if today was my last day, how would I behave? One thing is certain; we would see that our self-image was irrelevant, useless. We would dismiss a whole mountain of niggles and irritations, as we wouldn't have time for them. We'd see that anger and worry were pointless on this day, because they pollute the moment.

We might turn in the direction of some sensual pleasures, because although they can't be sustained for very long, they can enhance the moment. It's most likely that we would savour our time by satisfying ourselves that we really were here and now, looking at the garden, or talking to a friend. A cup of coffee would taste like no other.

The *scale* of everything we hold as important would change if this was our last day; it would shrink to what is at our fingertips. Getting a feel for the scope of that change can be quite instructive. The world is suddenly reduced under a zoom lens; not in the way of discarding it as unimportant (because we might decide we want to spend our moment reading about events in a distant land) but in focussing on what we regard as the priority for that moment; the flowers in the vase, a conversation with a loved one – or a report of a revolution abroad.

This, *if today were my last day,* mentality can be used on any day. It can remind us how far we are from enjoying the moment – and we can re-focus.

Now...

In any quiet moment, we can realise that all our life so far has come to *this* moment, everything we've done, everything we've ever been. We may have marched over deserts, climbed corporate mountains, made people laugh or cry, or led a very quiet, hardworking life, but there is only *now*.

Where are we? In the bath; having dinner with a friend; sitting in a doctor's surgery, or at our desk at the office. Who do we think we are at this instant, *now*? And we know that everybody else, whoever they think they are, only has this instant moment, a pulse this side of eternity. We can appreciate all that in this moment; we can look around, listen, smell the air, feel, *and be here and now.*

We can enrich this moment with thoughts of the past, we can ease the present moment and develop incentives for the future by planning for tomorrow; but it's common sense that we can't really 'live' at all unless we're conscious that we live in this moment, and we are focussed on it.

A meditative focus on the present

In many ways living in the moment is a meditative act. In meditation we learn to focus the mind. In being present here and now, we also have to focus the mind on how we want to use this moment. We put dishes in the wrong place when we're tidying the kitchen, because we're wondering if last night's dinner party was a success. We lose our way with our morning exercises, because we are thinking of our dispute with the brick-layer. We stop by the shelf in the supermarket, worried about what the doctor's report is going to say, and then ask ourselves what it was we wanted to buy.

The healthy mind has many thoughts running through it at the same time, and they pop into prominence often without being invited. Not only can this disturb our sleep, but it can spoil the taste of the here and now when we're awake. We are left in the confused area between two, or even three, separate thoughts with the frustrated feeling that we haven't dealt properly with any of them.

It's often not the relative importance of these different thoughts that matter. Small tasks like washing the dishes or watering the flowers can generate enjoyment when we concentrate on them. We have to decide that this is a moment to enjoy watering the flowers, and put off until later thoughts about how we're going to deal with the household bills. Effectively, we are saying to ourselves, 'I want to enjoy watering the flowers, and I'm going to devote this moment to the task. Other things can wait.' Living in the moment requires us to make an active selection of priorities.

It is a help to have it in mind that we have to check our sighting on the here and now, and maybe change priorities. What are we *really* doing? What do we *want* to do with this moment? That doesn't mean that we shouldn't think a number of different thoughts about past and future as we go through the day, and perhaps this story will make the point more clearly. A student once said to his guru, 'You taught us to think only of eating when we eat, but you are having breakfast *and* reading the newspaper.' The guru replied, 'When you decide to eat *and* read the newspaper, just do it.'

The 'now' is what we decide it is. If we want to think about a meeting we are going to have next week, that's our moment. If we want to enjoy our coffee, and take in the ambience of the coffee shop, that's our moment. What we want to avoid, is being borne along on a flow of disjointed and confused thoughts where the real moment is not enjoyed; it's clouded and half-experienced.

We *create* our own experiences

Our experience is that life can be chaotic and may even be unjust for many, but *we* have the option of giving it meaning, quite naturally, as we solve the problems of survival for ourselves in our own personal way. We can have whatever individual vocations, missions, goals or purposes we want. These are our 'meaning' and an expression of our survival instinct.

Our part in the creation of our own experience, and therefore in giving meaning to our activities, is the essential. Our moment is like a canvas, and on it we can paint any colours and shapes we want. We can be irritable and spoil the party, or we can be bright and celebrate it. We are not inert vehicles, mere conduits for the flow of life. We can and do create our life, and we are therefore responsible for its shape within the limits over which we have choice.

It's not what the moment *is,* because nothing really is – it's always what we *think* it is. A human being can be a skilful creator of his experience and meaning, and therefore enjoyment; or he can lapse into vacancy, bad temper and depression. Dejection, gloom and misery seem at times to reach out to us; we get to them effortlessly, we fall into their grasp without thinking. And the easiest option is often the one we take with little thought. But we have a choice, and it's a marvellous and energising choice!

Everybody has to accept the tide of unpleasant affairs, a storm, a company failure, a sudden illness, the loss of a loved one; but that does not mean that we lose the capacity to create the quality of the moment for ourselves. Indeed, our capacity to create and recreate ourselves in times of adversity is one of our best qualities. Our survival instinct is indomitable.

So what is actually meaningful?
It's impossible and unhelpful to make value judgments about what is meaningful to people. We have to look at it

personally. If we seriously believe something is meaningful, then it is, whether it is an act of creativity, working for a cause, loving somebody, doing a good job at work, ministering to others, climbing a mountain, or growing vegetables.

It's easy for us to undervalue the things other people regard as meaningful, because we see things from our own unique point of view. It was Voltaire's character Candide who, after searching the world to find out how to live, decided he should till his own garden. This is a metaphor which suggests that we should be focussing on what is within our reach now, and it implies the futility of looking over the fence and envying what the neighbours have.

A small and simple meaning perhaps?

Sometimes what is meaningful can be the enjoyment of just being here and now, looking at a view, or having a beer. There is no requirement for the meaning in our lives to be in some way 'significant'; it can be long or short term, important in the eyes of others, or very personal and private. Some people will play golf, collect ceramics, learn Spanish, chase butterflies, cultivate the garden, walk the hills, or simply read or write books. It's what they want to do; it engages them, and absorbs them; it has meaning for them. When we give meaning to an activity, we're shaping our life.

Meaning can exist whether we are comfortable, successful, rich, healthy, deprived, abused or disabled. If we look at the lives of some of the most gravely disabled people, we see that they are often rich with meaning.

Many of those who endured and survived concentration camps in the Holocaust probably found that a meaning, however limited, enabled them to survive.

The attraction of the exotic

We have so many choices in life for our pleasure that sometimes we're inclined to overlook the small things. A person may be more taken with the television screen than the view from the kitchen window, or with an exotic holiday abroad than a weekend at home. We tend to think in terms of a Hollywood spectacular, rather than the flowers in the park. And this is understandable because we like to be stimulated, and why not? But at the same time, we have to recognise that *this moment* is often composed of very small things – a conversation with a friend, an opportunity to make a decision, a chance meeting, a sudden sight of the sky, time watching an interesting film. In fact, most of life is composed of small things, however much we might wish for the spectacular; it's what is unfolding in front of us, literally before our eyes, and within our reach.

This consciousness of the small things which make up the now can give a sense of satisfaction, an understanding that instead of drifting in boredom or regretting yesterday, or hustling along in a swirl of thoughts about tomorrow, we are alive.

Is our existence meaningless?

It is difficult to get away from the existential position that everything *could* have been otherwise; a person could have been a carpenter in Sheffield instead of a doctor in

Dover; he could have been killed in a foreign war. He could have suffered a poor education, and spent a lot of time out of work. He could by chance have met a partner, and together they made a fortune. The cards have fallen this way rather than that. But if everything could have been different, it does not mean that the 'now' in which we all find ourselves is meaningless. It can have the meaning which we choose to give it.

Our 'now' is not merely a haphazard event, a chance roll of the dice in a chaotic and unpredictable world. We have no complete control over what happens to us, but we have some. Where each of us is now is the result of a very complicated chain of causation, some of which we will have set in train and for which we remain responsible. But we all have to face the element of the random and unpredictable in our lives. Does it matter? We just get on with it!

Meaninglessness is a powerful word which can depress us when it shouldn't. Our instinctive concern about meaninglessness may arise from living in an age focussed on the prime importance of us as individuals, and our self-actualisation. Our self-image, who we think we are, demands certainties which, as suggested in Chapter 1, are not attainable. We have our natural survival impulse to seek an understanding of the meaning of things, and a part of this is the assurance that we are well positioned and supported in a 'meaningful' and secure cosmic and earthly structure. This assurance is not attainable. We simply have to accept our positioning for what we know about it, and what it is.

The fact that we cannot know each other fully, or

determine our future in the cosmos, does not make our existence meaningless; these are limitations on us, yes, but no more than that. And from these limitations come very constructive and meaningful developments.

Our modest achievements mean something

If much about our life is random and unpredictable, and could have been otherwise, it cannot mean that everything a person has done(say twenty years in a steel foundry, or twenty years as a librarian) and everything he thinks he is, amounts to nothing. He has contributed to community life. He may have brought up a family, nursed a sick relative, become an expert billiards player, and collected Elvis Presley records. These activities are not meaningless. They are part, however small, of the vast surge for survival.

And most important, the time spent in the foundry or the library was not meaningless. All work, of whatever kind, has the special dignity we ought to attach to an individual sustaining himself; there is nobility in the human struggle for survival, and every worker however small contributes to it.

Living with our meaning

If we give the moments of our life meaning, we can live quite simply and happily. We have to recognise that when we say, 'the roses are beautiful,' or 'I love my child,' or 'I think a liberal democracy is the least worst political system,' that these are views that here and now have meaning for us, although in the unpredictable complex of existence they may mean little, nothing, or something entirely different.

If a person were to say, 'I'm not going any further. Life is meaningless. I might as well give up. I'll just lie down and die,' he would be denying his own nature. He would have lost the will to live. Our nature is that above all, we *want* to survive – but we also want secure, enjoyable lives. We want pleasure and love. We want happiness. Security, pleasure, love and happiness are not meaningless. The status of the cosmos doesn't make any difference to these powerful wants. They are feelings which are a real part of our lives and affect us every day.

We have vast scope in life to invest things, events and people with meaning.

What do we put our trust in?

The cultural barriers between people may be more formidable than the technical problems of travelling to Mars; but we can believe that reason, reasonableness, humanity, equality and freedom are likely to be guiding stars as knowledge deepens. In the ultimate, they are driven not by any religion or ideology, but represent a source for pragmatic solutions to the human problem of how to survive. Perhaps we are closer to understanding that the 'one size fits all' approach of ideology and religion just doesn't work.

To make room for other people's ideas, reason suggests that we need open societies where change can be the subject of rational reflection and action, rather than tribal impulses. Just as our personal self-interest often resists change, so community and national self-interest often presents a barrier to progress – but it is not too optimistic to hope that communities will yield to a degree in the interests of their better survival. And there can be no doubt that a calm and just community is integral to our personal happiness, because we are 'community' beings.

The psychonet and social development

In the discussion in Chapter 1, virtual reality (our assessment of what is going on outside us), was likened to a person using the internet. The connection between people and their knowledge was labelled the psychonet, on the analogy of an internet.

Human beings *and* their knowledge can be seen as one whole. Knowledge presupposes the existence of a human being who is able to know. What we know is part of us, and what we know collectively or have the ability to access is part of us all. This is not the collective unconscious which some psychologists write about, it is the collective conscious – a fact.

We seek to know, and we need to know and understand everything in the cosmos as part of our need to survive. Our personal search for knowledge may be petty compared to the scientist who unravels mysteries with the Hubble telescope, but our collective knowledge is developing every day. The speed of evolution of the psychonet is visibly much faster than genetic or geological evolution as a result of the pressure of human ingenuity.

Unthinkable and diverse progress has been made, particularly in the last hundred years, and not merely in science and technology. In economics, the fiction of the self-regulating global markets has been exposed. Politicians have invented numerous intergovernmental groups like the United Nations and the Arab League to discuss mutual problems, and the concept of concerted humanitarian help for nations that need it, is alive.

The evolution of the psychonet must be important for our survival, despite the fact that many of its products like nuclear weapons appear dangerous and threatening. Not all change progresses our survival. In the last century we have seen rapid scientific progress, while social and political advance has been dogged by deadly wars; but on balance there is every reason to hope that the psychonet will tend to produce a rational and accommodating pragmatism in our national as well as our personal affairs.

Are 'inalienable' human rights necessary for happiness?

The individual life is the only real life. The world exists only as far as it is reflected in the mind of the individual. In this sense, the individual observably has overwhelming primacy over everything that we know. He or she is unique and incomparable.

By contrast, the state, in order to measure and act upon its perception of community requirements, must reduce the individual to a statistic of relatively small importance. Human beings necessarily become quotas, numbers and percentages, they fall into categories and appear as a line of type on a list. The state aggregates people and delegates responsibility, subsuming individual judgments. We are governed.

The state may do many things with which we concur, but there is always the danger that the individual can be intimidated and victimised by the machine that he has created, for the very reason that he can only be seen by the state as a name in a register. There should therefore be a safeguard. This is the plain and simple case for human rights.

Although much has been written about 'absolute' or 'inalienable' human rights, it's clear that we only have the human rights granted to us by the state in which we live, and these may change from time to time. In fact there is nothing absolute or inalienable in our rights. What the state gives us, the state can take away – houses, bank accounts, open trials, the right to peaceful protest. For this reason, the state, whether it is a western democracy or not, ought to be treated with caution and regarded with healthy suspicion, as a juggernaut which has the potential power to crush the individual.

If we look at the problem this way, because some form of government is necessary, human rights are an *essential* bulwark for our survival, and, in this notional sense, ought to be treated as 'inalienable.'

Although conceivably a measure of peace and enjoyment can be found in our own back yard, it is precarious and seriously limited if there is no individual freedom and justice beyond our garden walls. As community creatures, we need to live in a just community.

Being part of the chaotic web of existence

We are left with the fact that we exist in, and as a part of, a web of relationships – family, friends, employment, community, nation and race. It's a rich, and very confused and chaotic web. And we can see that we are embedded in the whole animal and mineral existence of the planet, and beyond that, the universe. We can comprehend that we are a mere speck, but at the same time, an interdependent part of a great unity.

We are each a unique, tiny part of something immense and changing, which we can imagine as a oneness, a pattern of beauty perhaps, which we hardly understand. And there is every reason to accept, and rest easy in being part of the process of change, and the exciting adventures it promises.

From this perspective, life is a wonderful phenomenon to be observed, and lived for the meanings we can find, and for the meanings we can give it. There is no imperative that what we do should have an outcome, or a point, or be regarded as in any way important. Life can be a mystery to be experienced, a journey without a goal, other than the simple goals we set for ourselves on the way, for the purpose of our more effective survival.

Chapter 6

THOUGHTS ON HAPPINESS

This is a summary from the preceding pages:

1. Happiness, as distinct from pleasure, is a state of mind dependent upon an environment of peace and enjoyment. It's in our hands to create that environment.

2. That environment won't always be a harmonious external one, although that's what we try to create. It's also an environment of the mind, an attitude to life which enables us to deal effectively with external conflict.

3. Our happiness is related to who we think we are, because what we ask from life depends on who we think we are. Because we have no criteria for self-judgment, we have to be cautious about judging who we are. What we seek here is a sensible balance between what we want from life, and what we are likely to get.

4. We have a will to survive and prosper which is basically selfish, but if we want happiness, we have to be sufficiently enlightened to see that it must encompass genuine kindness and generosity to others.

5. An element of happiness is to be constantly aware of

the stabilising effect of understanding the unpredictability of life. An environment of peace and enjoyment can't be achieved without a tolerance of unpredictability.

6. More generally, acceptance and detachment can be cultivated as an attitude to life in everything that we do, and it can become a kind of tool to create the environment we seek.

7. The most important element of happiness is to be satisfied that we are engaged with life in ways we regard as meaningful.